Dead on Arrival:

How to Avoid the Legal Mistakes That Could Kill Your Start-Up

D0731535

First published by Dog Ear Publishing
4010 W. 86th Street, Ste H
Indianapolis, IN 46268
www.dogearpublishing.net

ISBN: 978-1-4575-0980-3

This book is printed on acid-free paper.

Printed in the United States of America

Preface

Dead on arrival ("DOA"). That is what many start-up companies are by the time the founders and promoters seek legal counsel—and even sometimes after being counseled—if they have not asked the right questions or sought the right type of attorney.

I have practiced law since 1984, primarily in the start-up company space. Throughout my career, I have seen engineers and very smart technical and business people leave their big company jobs to pursue great ideas. The minority of these people actually shepherd that idea to fruition. Many factors go into making a great start-up company and a founder must confront many challenges along the way.

Great legal advice will never ensure success for a company, but poor legal advice may result in failure. This book will help free the entrepreneur from legal headaches that result from being unaware of potential legal issues and pave the way to creating a great company.

This book is intended to be a guide for entrepreneurs on the legal traps and pitfalls to avoid. It lays out steps to take to ensure that your company is as well positioned for success as it can be as a legal matter and, most importantly, that the company's legal aspects are a nonissue for its stakeholders. The reader should consult this book not as a substitute for legal advice but as a guide to items that they should consider and matters that they should ask their attorneys to review. Each chapter in this book addresses a different important area of the law applicable to start-up companies. Each chapter is important. The well-advised entrepreneur should read the entire book before embarking on the start-up company journey.

A Note About Names

Throughout this book, I refer to actual persons and companies to illustrate my points. While the events are as accurately depicted as my memory will allow, unless otherwise expressly stated, all of the names have been changed, cleverly disguised, or made up so as to avoid the possibility of embarrassing anyone.

Chapter 1

Introduction

Scenario 1: You and your college buddy think up the next killer app while out at the bar one Friday night and write your idea on a napkin. You spend the next two years working nights and weekends writing code and preparing a business plan. You naturally assume that the company will be owned fifty-fifty and, in any case, you and your buddy will just work the details out later. After all, the product is what is important. Finally, you get to the point where you have a viable product and are ready to look for a financier, so you go to see a lawyer. That is when you first find out that your buddy has a much different view of what his equity ownership should be than you do. Your company is DOA.

Scenario 2: You have a full-time job at a big tech company in the Silicon Valley. One night, you think up a new product that is not related to your job, and you spend nights and weekends working on it. You also work on it during your lunch breaks and in your office at night on your employer's computer in your employer's office. It comes time to monetize your idea, and your employer reminds you of the standard invention assignment clause in your offer letter or proprietary information agreement. Your idea is DOA.

Scenario 3: You are a lot more sophisticated this time around and are not going to make any more rookie mistakes.

This time you see a lawyer and form a corporation. To keep things simple, when you do get an investor, you sell him or her common and not preferred stock and raise more money than you actually need. As a result, the founders have about 20 percent of the company, the investors have 80 percent, and you have not done your Series B round yet. You may not quite be DOA, but you definitely need major surgery.

Scenario 4: You sell common stock but only raise what you need to get to the next valuation milestone. When you decide to grant options, you find that the option price is the same as the price of the common stock, which is high since you sold common stock at a high price per share to raise money. The optionees do not feel too great about having high-priced options. Again, it may not be a DOA issue, but some expensive restructuring that easily could have been avoided is now required.

The above scenarios illustrate just a few of the common mistakes that start-up companies make on their path to liquidity. In all of these examples and in the dozens more to come in this book, we will examine winning legal strategies to position your company for success or, at least, to avoid setting it up for failure.

An entrepreneur should keep in mind the following three essential elements of a successful business: (1) people, (2) technology, and (3) money. I call it the "Success Triangle."

The people side of the triangle includes legal issues in connection with equity ownership, employment agreements, noncompetes (in some states), non-solicits, invention assignments, vesting, and immigration. The technology piece involves trademark, patent, copyright and other registrations, trade secret protection, nondisclosure agreements (NDAs), and intellectual property (IP) ownership. The money side involves financing and generating cash from operations.

A triangle is the strongest geometrical structure, but if there is a weakness in any of the three sides, the entire triangle will fail. So it is with the Success Triangle: one little mistake can weaken the entire structure. This book goes through the elements of each side and provides you with the information you should know and the questions you should ask your attorney—if he or she does not volunteer the information—to ensure that the triangle is as strong as possible.

This book is not focused on all the how-to's of company formation and financing. That is what lawyers are for. Instead, this book is focused on the mistakes that founders *and their lawyers* commonly make that result in a company being finished before it even starts, or DOA. And by DOA, here is what I mean:

1. A company that is not "fundable" (i.e., capable of attracting investment capital) is DOA. You might have the greatest idea in the world, but if no one will invest in it, it may be worthless.

2. A company that is insolvent is DOA. By insolvent, I do not mean technically insolvent (i.e., liabilities exceed assets). Almost every start-up is technically insolvent on formation. By insolvent, I mean that there is a substantial risk that the creditors will take all the value out of the company before the equity holders can realize on their investment.

3. A company that leaves no value for the residuary (i.e., the common stockholders) is DOA. In other words, if the capital structure (i.e., preferred stock) is set up in such a way that the common stockholders—usually being the service providers and founders—do not have a realistic possibility of making money on their stock when the company exits, the company is DOA.

4. A company that does not own its assets is DOA. Sounds axiomatic, doesn't it? But you would be surprised how often and easily this can happen.

5. A start-up company that is a defendant in material litigation may be DOA to an investor, unless the company's ultimate ability to prevail in the litigation is a sure thing.

At one step below DOA issues, there are what I call "valuation issues." A valuation issue is a defect or problem described above that is not so serious that it cannot be fixed or mitigated but will result in a significant reduction in valuation. For example, a company that is in litigation not significant enough to scare investors away still must reduce its valuation to account for the costs of the litigation.

Finally, there are mere "diligence issues," which include legal matters that have not been handled properly but can be remedied or fixed. Knowing the difference between the three types of issues is important, especially when it comes to "triaging" legal issues and allocating scarce resources. This book examines all three types of issues.

Chapter 2

Preformation and Formation

Usually, I represent companies but, sometimes, I represent founders.

On one recent occasion, I received a call from an individual who was quite upset about his "partners." He and two of his friends had been acting pursuant to a verbal partnership agreement for several months. Now that it was time to incorporate, the other two founders decided that my potential client was not right for their business. After talking with him for an hour I could see why, but my job is not to judge but rather to advocate, mediate, or pontificate.

The three founders held meetings, developed business plans, and wrote some code. Their verbal agreement was (allegedly) that the parties would each earn their shares in the company over time through continued service (commonly referred to as "vesting").

Based on this supposed vesting schedule, my client would have about 5 percent of the company's stock. Of course, none of this was in writing, and so the two other partners were taking the position that my guy had zero. The partners had a potential financier lined up and they were now incorporating. My client wanted to know what he was entitled to and what the other founders could do without him.

In answer to the first question, the possibilities are the following: (1) zero, because nothing is in writing; (2) one-third, because there are three founders; or (3) five percent, if that was the agreement on vesting.

If this were a law school exam question, I would probably pick the third possibility, but in the real world that is the wrong question to ask. The question of what my client was entitled to is academic until there is something behind the percentages. The more interesting question is the second question—what the other partners can do without him—or, to get to the nub of what he is really asking, "What can I demand from them?"

The practical answer is that they are screwed, a.k.a. DOA. There is, of course, nothing that prevents the partners from filing articles with the secretary of state forming the corporation and signing whatever documents issuing whatever stock they decide. They have the power to do that, but they might not have the right.

As a matter of theoretical rights, my client might have the right to a third of the business. Or five percent. Or something else. It would take a judge to tell us that after an expensive lawsuit, and as a practical matter, not many companies can get financed with the threat of litigation looming large. Thus, my client had tremendous leverage in this negotiation.

What should he do? What counteroffer should he make? I advised him that his opening move should be to convince his former partners to see a lawyer. They needed to understand the playing field. They did, and when they came back with their perfectly reasonable offer of five percent, we took it.

A less reasonable person might have gotten amnesia about the verbal vesting agreement and held them hostage for one-third, but we knew that would turn off an investor as much as the threat of litigation, since the company would need that common stock to replace my outgoing founder. We settled at five percent, the company was funded, and we are all waiting for an exit, so this story ends well. It might not have turned out that way.

Most mistakes are made at the preformation stage. Typically, one or more entrepreneurs have a great idea. One founder will be technical, and the other may have a business or marketing background. They plan to turn their idea into a product, market and finance it, sell it, get rich, and retire to the Bahamas.

The "partners" have a general understanding of how they are going to divide the business but commit nothing to writing and do not want to spend the money to form an entity to house the business. They have two sides of the Success Triangle and decide to formalize things when it is time to find an investor.

This illustrates the most common mistake that start-up entrepreneurs make—getting too far down the line with their idea while having no legal structure or agreement in place. Almost invariably, after an idea proves that it is going to be potentially successful, other players will start demanding more, and they have leverage because the company needs them to cooperate in order to get funding. So how do entrepreneurs protect themselves?

a. Pre-incorporation Agreements

I rarely advise clients to enter into a pre-incorporation agreement because it is duplicative of cost and effort when they eventually form an entity. The delay in entity formation may also result in the founders having to tell one more story to investors (more on this later)—i.e., why they have one extra step in their ownership trail.

More significantly, the agreement may place a few stakes in the ground on essential points but will not cover every issue without being a fairly extensive document. That may be enough to get started, but understand that there will still be points to cover.

Finally, if one founder changes his mind and decides that he will not honor the agreement, you may have every legal right to pay me a lot of your investors' money to shove that agreement down the founder's throat with a court action, but not many investors will want to invest in that lawsuit. If you are in that situation, you are DOA. My advice here is that if you have enough clarity to have a preformation agreement, skip the agreement and go straight to formation before people start changing their minds.

Not everyone will take that advice. So, for founders that do not incorporate right from the get-go, a preformation agreement is better than having nothing at all. In that case, at a minimum, here is what it should have:

i. Ownership Percentages. The number-one deal killer is the inability to agree on ownership. Get it in writing. There is no guarantee that your partners will not change their minds and refuse to sign their stock purchase agreements when it gets to that point, but at least you have legal rights as to ownership. If you have a hot enough company, you might just go forward on that basis if necessary.

ii. Vesting. Closely related to ownership percentages is the concept of "vesting." Here is how it works. The founders purchase their common shares for a small amount (since the company is new, it has a low valuation). If a founder leaves before a certain period of time has expired (usually three years in the Silicon Valley), the company may buy back the "unvested" shares at cost (not value). In effect, the founder loses those unvested shares. The repurchase right "lapses" (i.e., the shares "vest") over time so that, at the end of the period—say, three years—all of the shares are vested and not subject to repurchase. If the founder leaves after two years, two-thirds would be vested, and one-third would be unvested. You get the idea.

iii. Name. It sounds trite, but pick a name as soon as you can. You can always change it later—and odds are, you almost certainly will.

iv. Management Team. Years ago, three smart, young Stanford students with a great idea rushed to meet the venture capitalists (VCs) before they had their company formed. They also did not have a pre-incorporation agreement. They all gathered in my office with their slick PowerPoint slides and high collective IQs, ready to stun the world with their brilliance. The first question from the VC was, "Which of you will be the CEO?" and they all answered in unison, "Me." As comical as that was, it resulted in a short meeting and a healthy reality check as we went back, regrouped, and were better prepared the next time around. Do not let this happen to you. And by "management," I mean not only the officers—corporations usually require three offices to be filled: chief executive officer or president, chief financial officer or treasurer, and secretary—but I also mean the initial board of directors.

v. Type of Entity. Yes, you can figure this one out later, but the more specificity you have now, the better. Will it be a corporation or an LLC? If it is a corporation, will it be an S corporation or a C corporation? Oddly, the one question that seems to be the most mechanical is the one that entrepreneurs (and their lawyers) most often get wrong.

vi. Buy-Sell Provisions. Will there be a buy-sell agreement? What if someone dies? Becomes disabled? Moves to Tahiti? Can the company buy that person's shares back? At what price? About half of my start-up clients slow down enough to implement a good buy-sell agreement. All of them should.

vii. IP Ownership. In the "goes-without-saying" category, it is best to say it—the founders *must* assign (not license) all their rights to whatever gizmo is going to make their company great. If someone has the dumb idea that he or she will license and take the intellectual property back if things do not go well, you should know that early.

viii. Capital Contributions. How much cash are the founders going to kick in to get started? It could be almost nothing (and usually is) or there could be greater contribution expectations.

ix. Business of the Entity. What will the company's purpose be? Narrow or broad? The stated business purpose will make a difference when it comes to employment and related agreements.

x. Employment. Full-time or part-time? At what compensation level? Will salary be deferred?

xi. Other Issues. Now is the time to get everything out on the table. I prefer to work through a series of questionnaires to smoke out any "other issues," which are limited only by the imaginations of the dangerous minds that launch start-up companies. Do you expect the company to employ your girlfriend? Relocate to Nevada? Announce its allegiance to a cause, such as environmental awareness or healthy living? Don't laugh—I have seen all of these scenarios.

The idea of a pre-incorporation agreement has become less relevant recently as technology has taken much of the inefficiency out of incorporating. Companies such as Legal Zoom, Rocket Lawyer, and Nolo have commoditized entity formation and do it dirt cheap. Simply fill out a form and create your own legal documents. The reason they are so cheap is that they allow the customer and the technology to handle the routine aspects of the job, instead of an expensive attorney.

Our RoyseLaw Legal Wizard similarly contains a technology solution that allows parties to document their agreement without the expense of forming and maintaining an entity. Our system allows parties to act essentially as general partners until they are closer to viability. The system can be accessed at http://www.rroyselaw.com/ijuris_login_jp.html.

Basically, approved persons can create an agreement and an entity by answering a series of computer-generated queries. Unlike with other web based corporate solutions, a RoyseLaw Legal Wizard user will have access to legal advice if they request it. For example, a computer can generate corporate formation documents, but cannot tell you in the first instance what type of entity you should be. The RoyseLaw Legal Wizard allows access to legal advice from our law firm in addition to simple formation documents, and delivers an efficient legal solution at a fraction of the cost of forming corporations the old-fashioned way.

b. Protect Yourself from Your Current or Previous Employer

One common scenario is so pervasive that it deserves mention here. I am fortunate to practice law in California, which encourages innovation and entrepreneurship and discourages anything that affects the rights of employees to move freely. Here in the Silicon Valley, that attitude extends beyond the protections of the law and into the daily interactions of employees. Even lawyers jump ship frequently during their careers, and no one thinks the less of them for it. Nevertheless, even in this entrepreneur-friendly state, every start-up must consider the issue of whether it is starting out with trade secrets that belong to someone else—in particular, a previous employer.

After the former employee starts NewCo and quits his job, the entrepreneur's former employer may send a letter to the management of NewCo that says something to the effect of:

"Please take notice that [former employee] had access to valuable proprietary information that belongs to us, and if we find out that he is using our valuable proprietary information in his new position at NewCo, we will enforce our rights vigorously."

For the entrepreneur, the first lesson is, "Don't freak out." It is a standard letter—I have written it a hundred times. People expect it. It is just protection for OldCo. The appropriate response to OldCo (from NewCo's lawyer) will be something like this:

"Thank you for advising us of [former employee]'s obligations to OldCo. Of course, we would never dream of using OldCo's valuable proprietary information in NewCo's business. In fact, we are so mindful of this issue that we made [former employee] sign a statement saying that he has taken no valuable proprietary information from OldCo when he left."

By the way, the well-advised NewCo will in fact have that signed statement. It should be part of their employment documents.

And then you move on, unless, of course, the employee has downloaded a bunch of company files on his last day at OldCo's office. Then you have problems. The way to avoid those problems *is to not take any of OldCo's property*. That means do not download *anything*. Do not save any forms. Do not e-mail files to your home computer. If you do, you are asking for trouble. Remember, OldCo would like to see you fail. They want you to stay out of the market. The best way to do that is to convince your investors that all the money they give to you will be given to me to defend you when OldCo sues you. Don't give them that opportunity, or you will be DOA.

c.   Choice of Entity

One of the first legal issues an entrepreneur is confronted with is what type of entity they should form, and it is surprising how often they get it wrong, even with (and sometimes especially because of) legal counsel. The problem is compounded by the availability of cheap online "do it yourself" incorporation solutions. Many companies will give you all the documents and forms needed to create an entity, but will not tell you which type of entity you should be (or in which state or country you should locate), since that would be the unauthorized practice of law.

There is an old joke about a consultant who is hired to shut off an imploding nuclear reactor by pressing the correct sequence of control panel buttons. "How much do you charge?" ask the owners. "Only $50 to press the button," replies the consultant, "but $1 million to know which button to press." Many of the non-lawyer services will help you push the button, but will not tell you which button to push.

As discussed above, the RoyseLaw Legal Wizard also allows clients to inexpensively create entities and takes much of the inefficiency out of the process by allowing clients to do much of the work themselves, but with the added benefit of attorney review. The RoyseLaw Legal Wizard reserves to licensed attorneys the aspects of the process that require a lawyer. The RoyseLaw Legal Wizard process will tell you which button to push.

It is helpful to start off with a basic description of the different types of entities the businessperson can form:

Sole Proprietorship. This is the simplest and easiest form of doing business. It means that one person is doing business by himself, with no entity protection. The entrepreneur might publish a local notice that he is using a fictitious business name (a d/b/a), but that is generally about it. The benefit of this form of doing business is simplicity and cost. There is no entity and thus no cost. Accountants sometimes suggest doing business this way to avoid paying the costs of formation and the costs of preparing tax returns for a separate entity.

The most obvious downside of this type of business is that there is no liability protection. If the entrepreneur owns a corporation, for example, and the corporation conducts a business that ends up getting sued, the liability of the corporation can end at the corporate level, and the owner/entrepreneur can, in general and subject to exceptions, avoid liability for corporate debts. The most common response to this argument is that the entrepreneur can insure against most of the tort liability that he might attract. While this is theoretically true, the fact that the entrepreneur has insurance coverage does not mean that he need not defend against a claim. It just means that he can try to get his insurer to defend for him.

More to the point, it is often said that insurance companies are not in the business of paying claims. They are in the business of denying them, and there is always the possibility that the insurer will deny coverage, leaving the entrepreneur bare. Because of this issue, most entrepreneurs would not remain sole proprietors for long. Think of the costs of forming and maintaining an entity as an insurance premium to insulate the entrepreneur from business liabilities.

Partnership. If more than one entrepreneur decides to act without the liability shield of a corporation or LLC (see below), they will likely be acting as general partners, meaning that each partner can bind the other to the debts and obligations of the business. This form of doing business has all the problems of a sole proprietorship, with the added burden of having to file tax returns. In addition, the partners should have a partnership agreement between them defining their roles and responsibilities, thus defeating much of the cost savings that they hoped to achieve by avoiding a limited liability entity. In addition, some states (like California) have a state filing for general partnerships, so not much in the way of cost is saved by being a general partnership as opposed to an LLC or a corporation (other than annual minimum taxes of $800 per year in California).

Limited Partnership. A limited partnership is a partnership in which the "limited" partners have very little role in management but are not liable for the debts and obligations of the partnership (beyond their contributions or contractual agreement to make contributions). A limited partnership must have a "general" partner who manages the partnership's business and is fully liable for all the debts and obligations of the partnership. A limited partnership is commonly used for investment vehicles, such as private equity funds, real estate, and R&D partnerships, but is rarely used for operating companies since the arrival of the limited liability company (LLC) described below. A limited partnership is relatively inefficient because in the typical limited partnership structure, the general partner wishes to avoid having general liability so it will hold its general partnership interest through a corporation or other limited liability entity. Thus, the use of a limited partnership usually requires the formation of two entities instead of one to attain liability protection—the whole point of an entity to start with.

Limited Liability Company (LLC). The LLC is a relatively recent form of business entity in the United States and is steadily gaining acceptance as an appropriate vehicle even for operating companies. Basically, an LLC is a company in which no member has personal liability for the debts and obligations of the company (other than as agreed).[1] The management of the LLC is vested in a manager, a managing member, or all the members as set forth in an operating agreement. The LLC is taxed like a partnership (unless otherwise elected), meaning that its income "passes through" and is picked up on the returns of its members in such proportions as is set forth in the operating agreement, subject to the limitations of the Internal Revenue Code and regulations.

The beauty of an LLC is that it is amazingly flexible and can accommodate almost any deal that the parties can think up. The downside of an LLC is that it is amazingly flexible, and every LLC operating agreement must address all the deal points that the parties wish to negotiate. The flip side of flexibility is complexity, and the more tailored the operating agreement is, the more complicated it can become. This is not usually a deal breaker, but it is a point to be aware of.

The tax advantage of an LLC over a C corporation cannot be overstated. A C corporation is subject to two levels of taxation: once when it earns income and again when it distributes

---

[1] Watch out for this. Many off-the-shelf, boilerplate LLC operating agreements have an unlimited "deficit restoration provision," which means that the LLC members must contribute to the LLC to the extent that they have a negative capital account. Many LLC members have discovered that they had to come out of pocket on liquidation of the LLC as a result of imprudent drafting.

that income as a dividend to its shareholders. Since start-ups do not usually pay dividends—if you do, you do not need VC funding—this issue looms largest in connection with the sale of the company.

Upon a sale of all the company's assets, the LLC members could get away with a federal rate of tax of 15 percent (as of this writing) on all the gain from the sale of capital assets. Ignoring for a moment the tax exclusion of gain from a sale of qualified small business stock treatment (see below), that same sale conducted through a C corporation could result in a federal tax of 35 percent at the corporate level and another 15 percent at the shareholder level. Add state taxes on top of that, and you can see the size of the disparity (potentially 56% vs. 25%).[2] Obviously, the calculation is more complex than that, and you might wonder why many start-up company lawyers do not recommend an LLC for every start-up company. There are a few reasons why the LLC form of doing business has not gained widespread acceptance as an appropriate structure for a company that intends to solicit VC financing (at least, not in my Silicon Valley neighborhood).[3]

First, the tax provisions can be complex, and many lawyers who deal in start-ups do not have the expertise to advise on, or draft, LLC operating agreements. The LLC form of doing business is not within their comfort zone.

---

[2] Based on tax rates in effect as of the date of this writing, one level of tax subjects the gain to a tax rate of roughly 25 percent in California (assuming a federal long term capital gains rate of 15 percent). Two levels of tax result in about a 42 percent blended rate at the corporate level (35 percent federal plus 9 percent state tax, which is deductible for federal income tax purposes), and another roughly 25 percent at the shareholder level. Thus, if a corporation sells all its zero basis assets for $100, it pays $42 in tax and distributes $58 to its shareholders. If the shareholders have no basis in their shares, they pay another $14 on the $58 distribution, resulting in $56 of the $100 going towards taxes.
[3] Losses also pass through to members, but in the real world, they are often limited either by the basis limitations or the passive activity rules of Internal Revenue Code section 465.

Second, and more importantly, most VC funds will not invest in an LLC. Their reluctance to invest is due to the fact that income and loss passes through to them and, in turn, passes through to their investors. If the VCs' investors are foreigners or tax-exempt entities, they end up with a US tax liability that they probably do not want to have. In fact, a typical venture fund partnership agreement will have representations and warranties that the fund will avoid investing in anything that would result in that type of income.[4]

Third, and perhaps less significant to all but those of us who wallow in this area, a compensatory "option" on an LLC interest can be complex and problematic (and cannot qualify as tax-favored incentive stock options or ISOs). Thus, LLCs often grant a "profits interest" instead of an option to service providers. A profits interest entitles the holder to a share of profits and/or appreciation in value after the date of grant. The grant of the interest is nontaxable under current IRS guidance, but does require the company to tell the grantees a story that would not need to be told with an option plan. That story includes a mention of the fact that they will receive an IRS Form 1065, Schedule K-1, reporting their shares of the income and loss of the company on their individual tax returns. Hopefully, they will have a good tax preparer that is familiar with LLCs. As a result of these concerns, the use of compensatory bonus plans is becoming increasingly popular, but they raise their own issues.

This dynamic presents each founder with a dilemma: either (1) form an LLC and get a good tax result but disqualify the company from VC investment, or (2) form a corporation and get a potentially lousy tax result but start with a simple, fundable structure. Although this may seem like a real head-scratcher, there is an easy solution.

Assuming careful drafting at the outset, an LLC can easily convert to a corporation. The reverse is not true—changing

---

[4] For those of you who are curious, the troublesome types of income are "effectively connected income" for foreigners and "unrelated business taxable income" for tax-exempts.

from a corporation to an LLC is a potentially taxable event. The incorporation of an LLC is almost always tax free as a "351 transaction" (referring to section 351 of the Internal Revenue Code)[5] and can be accomplished in many states with the filing of a single piece of paper with the relevant secretary of state in a statutory "conversion." Thus, one plan is to form the company initially as an LLC and bake the incorporation procedures into the operating agreement so that the company is teed up to incorporate when necessary.

Having organizational documents that anticipate the incorporation is important to avoid later disputes about who gets what stock, as well as for securities law reasons (see the discussion of Rule 144 below). This is a strategy that we regularly employ (through the RoyseLaw Legal Wizard) unless the company will have nonresident alien members (who do not want to get caught in the US tax system)[6] or if the founders are absolutely, positively sure that they will solicit private equity investment very early in the company's life and will have to unwind the whole thing soon anyway.

Choosing the wrong entity may not be a DOA problem, but may be a thirty-percentage-point tax problem. If your investor is marginal on the investment decision and is a tax-sensitive angel or strategic investor, it very well may be a DOA problem.

C Corporation. The vast majority of new companies are formed as a corporation—partly due to simplicity and partly due to the fact that most VCs can and will invest only in C corporations. The reference in this section to C corporations is intended to distinguish this type of corporation from a corporation that has made an election to be taxed under Subchapter S

---

[5] For the tax geeks in the reading audience, you may visit Rev. Rul. 84–111 for a description of the three ways that LLCs can incorporate and the potentially different results under each method.

[6] Even in this case, there are ways to "block" the nonresident alien's US tax obligations and the LLC's corresponding withholding obligations, but it may be more hassle than it is worth..

of the Internal Revenue Code (see below). As a state law matter, there is no difference between a C corporation and an S corporation.

The benefit of a corporation is that many of those highly flexible provisions of an LLC operating agreement are set forth by statute or outlined in a standardized boilerplate set of bylaws. The shareholders of a corporation have limited liability and have the rights to vote and participate only as set forth in the bylaws, by statute, or by shareholders' agreement. Generally, the management of the company is delegated to a board of directors, who further delegates the day-to-day business to the officers. The corporation should have (and under some state laws *must* have) at least three officers: a president or CEO, a treasurer or CFO, and a secretary. The same person can hold all three offices.

A C corporation is a separate taxable entity, as discussed above. One tax benefit of a corporation is that it can participate on a tax-free basis in a stock swap. In other words, an acquisition of a corporation in a stock-for-stock exchange may be nontaxable. An acquisition of an LLC in a corporate stock (of the acquirer) for interests in the LLC exchange will usually be taxable to the exchanging holders of LLC interests.[7] C corporation shareholders do not receive IRS Form 1065 Schedule K-1, so they do not have to worry about paying tax on the income of the entity like members of an LLC do, and equity compensation plans (stock options) are less complicated in a corporate context.

Another tax benefit of a C corporation is that gain from the sale of C corporation stock might qualify for exemption or rollover of gain if the stock is qualified small business stock. Fifty percent of the gain realized on the sale of certain qualified small business stock ("QSBS") held for at least five years may be exempted from income for federal tax purposes. QSBS, subject to a few exceptions, means stock in a domestic corporation if:

---

[7] The parties may be able to structure around a taxable result in the case of an acquisition of an LLC by a corporation, but the direct exchange of LLC interests by LLC members for stock in a corporation will usually be taxable.

(1) such corporation is a "qualified small business" ("QSB") at the time the stock is issued; and (2) the taxpayer acquires the stock, in an original issuance of such stock, in exchange for money, other property, or as compensation for services to the issuing corporation.

In general, a QSB is a domestic C corporation, with $50 million or less in gross assets (without regard to liabilities), that is engaged in an "active business" (i.e. cannot be an investment company). The Section 1202 exclusion for a taxpayer is limited to the greater of (i) $10 million or (ii) ten times such taxpayer's basis in the QSBS. However, because of the alternative minimum tax (AMT), a taxpayer subject to AMT would end up with nearly the same tax liability, regardless of such taxpayer's election to exclude gain under Section 1202.[8] A taxpayer may also elect to roll over capital gains from the sale of QSBS held for more than six months if other small business stock is purchased by the individual during the sixty-day period beginning on the date of sale.

If the company is formed as a corporation, here are some traps to avoid:

Board of Directors. Before your company is financed, the board should have three members at most. If you must have more than three board members, make sure people understand that they will be coming off the board when the company is

---

[8] The Small Business Jobs Act of 2010 ("SBJA 2010") provides for an exclusion of 100 percent of the gain realized on the sale of certain qualified small business stock ("QSBS") held for at least five years, if such QSBS is acquired or issued between September 27, 2010 and January 1, 2011. In certain cases involving Empowerment Zones, the exclusion is increased to 60 percent, and for QSBS acquired or issued between February 17, 2009 and September 28, 2010, the federal government increased the exclusion to 75 percent. SBJA 2010 not only increases the Section 1202 gain exclusion to 100 percent, but removes the excluded gain from the list of AMT tax preference items. Therefore, a taxpayer electing for exclusion under Section 1202 will have a zero federal tax liability with respect to the sale of QSBS held for at least five years, if such QSBS is acquired or issued between September 27, 2010 and January 1, 2011.

financed. There is a temptation in closely held companies to give everyone management participation rights. The danger is that you must then create a successively larger board with each new stakeholder. The result may be a board that is cumbersome and hard to manage. Stick with three.

Bylaws and Shareholder Agreements. The more standard, the better. More than once, I have been involved in transactions where some clever lawyer decided to bake a right of first refusal or some other shareholder-friendly provision into organizational documents, only to cause a lot of last-minute angst in an attempt to close a financing or sale. Do not plant any time bombs that might be overlooked until it is too late, especially things that require anyone's consent to waive. Sometimes, that consent comes at a cost. The documents should be "plain vanilla."

Buy-Sell Agreements. A buy-sell agreement is an agreement among stockholders to sell their shares of stock to the company (and possibly the other shareholders) upon the occurrence of certain events. A buy-sell agreement is generally a good idea, but keep in mind that it has to allow for the necessary flexibility to go from a closely held to a financed or sold company.

The one example that seems to come up again and again is a right of first refusal that extends not only to the company but also to the shareholders. This is a great idea in a family-owned business that will always be closely held, but it is a bad idea for a company from which the founders will want to exit at some point. Why? Because the right of first refusal gives each shareholder a right to buy the company or its securities before a third party can, which will chill any potential offers. Who wants to go through the trouble of doing diligence if one of the existing shareholders is just going to match the offer and buy the company or the offered securities anyway? The same comment applies to preemptive rights and rights to maintain. Be careful with boilerplate provisions that work with closely held companies, unless of course you want to spend the rest of your life being in an illiquid, closely held company.

S Corporation. The S corporation is my favorite. It is a corporation under state law, so it is relatively simple to form (i.e., inflexible). The S corporation is a "pass-through" for federal income tax purposes, and so it offers tax advantages over the C corporation. The S corporation form also allows for more traditional corporate equity compensation, such as an option plan (see below), and it can be a party to a tax-free, stock-for-stock merger or exchange.

The downsides are that an S corporation can have only one class of stock (i.e., no common and preferred stock structure), all of its shareholders must be individuals who are US citizens or residents (for tax purposes), and it is limited to one hundred shareholders (hardly ever a real concern in the start-up company world). Thus, a VC or other institutional investment will terminate the S election, but the shareholders may enjoy the benefits of pass-through treatment until then (like tax losses, subject to limitations). Unlike an LLC, the distribution of property from the corporation to its shareholders (on liquidation, for example) is a potentially taxable event.

I would suggest an S corporation to a company that wants to stay as close to a traditional option plan as possible or expects its exit to be a stock-for-stock merger or exchange. If an S corporation does adopt a traditional option plan, it must take care to build provisions into its plan that prevent a termination of its S election. Unfortunately, most option plans miss this point entirely.

Phantom or incentive plans are often used in an S corporation context to avoid the shareholder limitations problem. Sometimes, an S corporation will have both an option plan and an incentive plan. Phantom plans are described in more detail later. For now, just know that they work elegantly in an S corporation environment for rewarding employees.

An S corporation should also have a good shareholders' agreement ensuring that the company makes "tax payment distributions" to the shareholders to cover their taxes. The agreement should restrict the shareholders from transferring their shares or taking any other action that would terminate the S election without the consent of a specified percentage of the shareholders.

An S corporation is subject to another trap that often results in disaster. Since an S corporation can only have one class of stock, it cannot issue preferred stock to angel investors. Thus, it might decide to sell common stock to investors. This is a terrible idea. The sale of common stock will result in setting a higher price on the company's common stock than it would have had if the company had instead sold preferred stock. That high price will make options (which must be exercisable at fair market value at grant) unattractive. The Silicon Valley game exploits the disparity in value between common and preferred stock (which is worth more because of its preferences, sometimes up to ten times more). That game is gone when common stock is sold for cash.

The other—and more significant—consequence of selling common stock is that it necessarily results in the founders giving up too much of the company to the angel investors. If the value of the stock is low, the company must sell more stock to raise the same dollars. Because preferred stock is priced higher than common, the company gets more bang for the buck by selling preferred stock to investors.

Because of those concerns, an S corporation will often issue convertible debt to angel or early investors. The debt will convert to stock issued in the next financing at a discount to the valuation established in that round. The beauty of this instrument (for both S corporations and C corporations) is that it defers the valuation question to the institutional round, while giving the early investors a benefit for investing early (the discount). Be careful, however. S corporations may only have one class of stock, and while straight debt is not a second class of stock for this purpose, convertible debt does not fall into an IRS "straight debt safe harbor" exception to the one class of stock rules. If the debt converts to common stock at a discount to fair market value, the IRS may view the debt as a separate class of stock, resulting in a termination of the S election. Careful planning is required to avoid this adverse result. The takeaway lesson is that tax advice must go into almost every step of the S corporation formation and financing process.

Other Entities. Some other entities are rarely (but sometimes) used as start-up company vehicles. One such entity is the business trust. One of the definitional characteristics of a trust is that it is formed to hold or preserve property. Some states—Delaware, for example—authorize the formation of a trust (a "business trust") to conduct a business. The business trust can be an appropriate vehicle for a syndicated investment program in, for example, real estate properties, but it is almost never the right answer for an operating start-up company.

Similarly, nonprofit and not-for-profit companies are not suitable entities as a definitional matter. With the increased interest in socially responsible or "green" investing, many states are considering, or have enacted, legislation that would allow corporations to consider social goals as part of their mandate. California, for example, recently enacted legislation that allows the creation of Benefit Corporations and Flexible Purpose Corporations. Both are designed to allow corporations to act in a socially responsibly way while maximizing shareholder wealth, but they are slightly different. The board of directors of a Benefit Corporation is required to take the environment, community, employees, and suppliers into account. The Flexible Purpose Corporation allows a corporation to select a specific mission, such as a charitable or public purpose.

Foreign Corporations. A few words should be said about foreign corporations. More and more, US investors are getting comfortable investing in foreign companies. The main reason people mention foreign corporations is that they may have heard that they can avoid US taxes by forming their entity in a foreign tax haven. Sometimes they can, but they should consider that a domestic institutional investor will have a strong preference for investing in a Delaware corporation over a foreign corporation due to familiarity with, and certainty of, US law. Nevertheless, a company may have legitimate reasons for incorporating in a foreign jurisdiction ("offshore"). Properly structured, the use of a foreign corporation may avoid US taxation on its earnings until those earnings are paid or "repatriated" to its US owners. Thus, the foreign corporation could grow and reinvest its earnings offshore on a tax-free or tax-reduced basis.

First and foremost, US investors prefer US companies. They understand US companies and can see the US exit, especially if that exit is an initial public offering (IPO) on a US exchange. That is not to say that US investors will not invest in a foreign corporation—more and more, they do—but the company must have good reasons for going offshore, and the structure must actually work. Notwithstanding the tax advantages, the whole world effectively accepts Delaware corporations as established, credible investment entities. Thus, establishing an offshore corporation might be the most efficient thing as a tax matter but not the thing that is most likely to get you funded.

If you still want to be offshore, here is a brief summary of the opportunities and pitfalls.

The rule that will shoot most of these ideas down before they even get started is that foreign corporations are taxable in the United States on their income that is "effectively connected" with a US trade or business ("ECI").[9] In other words, if the foreign corporation intends to conduct a US trade or business, organizing as a foreign corporation will not avoid US tax on that business's income. Corporations organized in countries with which the US has an income tax treaty enjoy the benefit of a higher standard, and are not taxed on US business income unless that income is attributable to a permanent establishment.

What about intellectual property (IP)? The popular press likes to pick on IP holding companies from time to time. An IP holding company is a foreign company (usually organized in a tax

---

[9] A US trade or business means regular, substantial and continuous profit oriented activities in the U.S. *Comm'r v. Spermacet Whaling & Shipping Co.*, 281 F.2d 646 (6th Cir. 1960).

haven) that is formed to hold intellectual or intangible property rights (like patents or trade secrets), which it then licenses to operating company affiliates. The advantage, when it works, is that the income from the exploitation of the IP is earned by a foreign (and not US) corporation and thus is not taxed by the United States until it is actually paid to a US company. Similarly, a company may put more than IP into a foreign corporation with the same idea—to avoid US tax on the earnings of the company.

Assuming that a company can avoid having ECI, income from IP might not escape US tax if the IP is licensed for use in the United States. In that case, the United States will impose a 30 percent withholding tax on the US-source royalties, unless that rate is reduced by an income tax treaty. For obvious reasons, the United States is not a party to tax treaties with tax haven countries where a company would want to establish an IP holding company.

If the IP will not result in US-source income (i.e., will not be licensed to US licensees), the income might still be taxable back to the US owners of the foreign corporation under one of the United States' antideferral regimes. In a typical IP holding company structure, the foreign company will hold and license the IP to an affiliate, thereby generating royalty income. Alternatively, it might conduct manufacturing and sales through contract manufacturers.

First, if the foreign corporation is more than fifty percent owned by US persons (ten percent US shareholders), the US shareholders must include their pro rata share of the corporation's "Subpart F income" in taxable income on an annual basis, as if the company declared dividends each year. For an IP holding company, Subpart F income will usually catch passive (but not active) royalties.

If the foreign corporation is not more than fifty percent owned by US persons but is a passive foreign investment company (PFIC), then the US shareholders must include their pro rata shares of passive income in their income, whether or not it is distributed. A foreign corporation is a PFIC if 75 percent or more of its gross income for the taxable year is passive, or if at least fifty percent of its assets during the taxable year produce passive income or are held for the production of passive income.

The annual taxable income inclusions reduce the benefits of a lot of the IP holding company structures, as well as the foreign operating company structures that do not have the ability to actually place economic processes offshore. In addition, even if the group has the metrics to benefit from the use of a foreign IP holding company, the transfer of technology to the offshore company can be problematic. A contribution of technology to a corporation can often be accomplished tax free. A tax-free contribution of intangible property, such as technology, to a foreign corporation, however, may implicate the "super royalty rules" that impute annual US income inclusions that are "commensurate with the income from the intangible."[10] A "sale" of the IP at fair market value to the foreign corporation would avoid annual US income inclusions that are "commensurate with the income from the intangible," but that sale might trigger immediate taxable income.

As is apparent, international planning is easier earlier in a company's life because there is less value to move around in a taxable manner. However, *earlier* is not a great option for a cash-strapped start-up that does not have $25,000–$100,000 to plan and set up international operations. As a result, these structures do not always get off the drafting table.

Obviously, international tax planning is vastly more complex than the short outline given here. You can read about foreign tax planning in the articles cited on our website at http://www.RoyseUniversity.com, or instead spend your time doing something that may generate revenue for your start-up. In any case, the takeaway here is that good tax counsel is essential if you are thinking of doing anything international.

State of Formation or Incorporation. Finally, a few words are in order about the state of formation or incorporation. As

---

[10] IRC section 367(d).

mentioned above, Delaware is the jurisdiction of choice for corporations and LLCs. This choice of jurisdiction is typically justified on the basis that Delaware law contains more certainty than other states' law since there is a large body of Delaware case law. The Chancery Court of Delaware is reputed to enforce documents as written more than many other states. In addition, many lawyers believe that Delaware law offers more protection to directors in cases of shareholder suits. Ironically, Delaware law arguably offers *less* protection than some states to a director in the case of a suit by creditors against an insolvent corporation alleging breach of fiduciary duties.[11] This is not insignificant, since many start-ups are technically insolvent right from the start, and many more end up there.

Delaware does not impose a tax on income for companies that are incorporated but not doing business in Delaware, but it does impose a franchise fee measured by par value or assumed par value of capital. The calculation of the Delaware franchise tax can be a subtle "gotcha" and may result in a large amount of tax when a small amount would have been due with only slightly different drafting.

Most significantly, Delaware is the jurisdiction of choice for the VC community[12], and VCs will often require a corporation to reincorporate in Delaware as part of its financing. This is generally not a big deal, but companies that know that they will be soliciting institutional funding may as well incorporate in Delaware since they will probably migrate there anyway.

---

[11] Compare *Berg & Berg Enterprises, LLC v. Boyle*, 178 Cal. App. 4th 1020 (2009) (director has no fiduciary duty to corporate creditors when the corporation is in "zone of insolvency") with *Credit Lyonnais Bank Nederland, N.V. v. Pathe Communications Corp.*, 1991 WL 277613 (Del. Ch. Dec. 30, 1991) (director's fiduciary duty expanded to include creditors if the corporation is insolvent or in the "vicinity of insolvency").

[12] Unlike other states, Delaware does not require class voting on issues such as a merger or acquisition, so the common stockholders may not be able to block a merger of a Delaware corporation that the VCs approve in circumstances in which they would be able to block a merger of the corporation if it were organized under the laws of another state.

Nevada is often mentioned as a favorable jurisdiction in which to incorporate. Because Nevada has no income tax and has a relatively simple corporate code, many companies incorporate in Nevada. Many publicly traded or pink-sheet-listed companies are formed under Nevada law. Some practitioners believe that Nevada will become the new Delaware, mostly due to Delaware's aggressive enforcement of its "gotcha" franchise tax system. Although it does not yet carry the cache of Delaware as a choice of jurisdiction, Nevada is a perfectly acceptable jurisdiction of formation for all of the corporate reasons listed above. It is not a good choice as a jurisdiction of formation if the objective is to avoid taxes *unless* the company can locate property, employees, or sales in Nevada. State tax is imposed based on economic factors—not on which state's name appears on the company's charter. If the company's business operations are located in a state other than Nevada, forming under Nevada law will not result in a substantial tax savings. If, however, the company's officers move to Nevada or the company locates its offices or physical facilities in Nevada, then some or all of the company's income will be apportioned away from other (taxable) states and allocated to Nevada (a no-tax state), thereby reducing the group's overall tax liability. This is an often-cited reason that companies move from California to Nevada for tax savings (and other incentives).

A company may form an affiliate under the law of a low or no tax state, such as Nevada and Delaware. The low-taxed, or untaxed, company may hold technology and license that technology to the group's affiliates in taxable states. The royalties paid by the taxable companies to the nontaxed companies may be state tax deductible and reduce the taxable income of the taxed company. Those royalties correspondingly increase the income of the untaxed company without a tax consequence. This strategy is designed to reduce the overall rate of tax on the group.

Locating within Nevada for tax reasons may be worth considering, but, of course, the issue is not quite that cut-and-dried.

California, for example, has adopted a unitary business taxation concept that, basically, will evaluate the apportionment factors of all members of the unitary group, in effect ignoring the IP holding company structure. An analysis of whether the members are engaged in a unitary business is thus required before implementing such a structure.

By this time, you should be getting a sense as to why start-up companies often do not expend the substantial effort required to analyze state-income-tax-saving legal structures when there are limited dollars and seemingly unlimited demands on those dollars. Structures should not be based on tax reasons without thoughtful and competent tax advice. Being incorporated in the wrong state or for the wrong reasons may not be a DOA issue, but it will be a distraction when the company must migrate to another jurisdiction.

d. Do-It-Yourself Formations

As easy as it is to do, entity formation involves some real traps that extend beyond the choice of entity decision. The following brief story about the CEO of one of my clients illustrates the dangers of fast, cheap, and easy ventures. I call it...

How to Save $1,000 in Legal Fees. Peter sat back in his chair and smiled at the annual report to investors for fiscal year 2001. The complex Excel spreadsheet had shown again that Peter was an exceedingly smart businessman. In the almost twenty years since he had assumed management of his fund's real estate portfolio, he had consistently outperformed the market and brought huge returns to his investors. He managed to do this consistently by applying an economic system that he had devised while teaching a college class in economics. The plan involved buying and leasing to stable retail businesses on a triple-net basis, and it had proven spectacularly successful, weathering even the recession following the 9/11 attacks.

The only problem with the program was that the returns, while sure and steady, were not large compared to what could be earned in more risky investments, such as commercial development. Knowing the potential returns, Peter was keenly interested when approached by a developer to get in on the ground floor of some multiuse development projects in the Pacific Northwest. If the projects hit their numbers, their short-term returns would dwarf the slow and steady returns of the past twenty years.

Of course, real estate development was much different from passive investing and leasing, but if the past twenty years had shown anything, they had shown that Peter was smart—much smarter than the average real estate fund manager and certainly smarter than the rubes that had presented him with the opportunities in Portland and Seattle. If those guys could make a profit at this game with their rudimentary skills and lack of economics training, Peter would hit home runs.

Not only was Peter a brilliant businessman and economist, he also was extremely adept at handling his own documents—tax and legal. As an academic, he was very good at learning about things that were outside his area, and he never relied on legal counsel for anything but the most routine real estate matters. Thus, when it came time to negotiate the LLC operating agreement for his fund's investment in the developments, Peter took a first pass at the documents himself.

When Peter finally did come to me, at the insistence of his investors, he was much more interested in what the cost of my review would be than the actual product. He intended to invest about $2 million of his fund's close to $20 million of value in the first project, so did not want to spend too much on legal review. After some haggling, I quoted Peter a flat $1,000 to review the agreement for high-level issue spotting.

In Peter's mind, he was only asking for my help because his investors had pestered him about it. He viewed himself as being much smarter than I—that is why he was the client, and I was merely the lawyer. Nevertheless, I suggested that he take me up on my offer to review his agreement, and he politely declined. He would handle this small matter himself.

You can probably guess what happened next. The LLC agreements had an unlimited capital call provision, meaning that the projects *and their creditors* could call capital from the investors beyond their initial investment to whatever extent needed. Peter did not worry too much about that provision since his fund had relatively small percentages. What he did not realize is that every other investor in the deal invested through a special purpose entity, as would be prudent in an investment such as this. I can still recall the look on Peter's face when I told him that his $2 million investment accompanied $80 million of capital call liability, far in excess of all his fund's assets and all of its gains for the past twenty years. With a single pen stroke, Peter had wiped out twenty years of gains. But it got worse.

One of the projects went into bankruptcy. The others ended up in several federal and state court lawsuits. Peter was sued personally for his negligence. The whole mess did not get settled until many years later.

The last time I saw Peter was when he came to pay his final invoice to me for assisting in the cleanup. As he wrote the check, he mentioned that not only did he lose a bundle on the investments, but his investors had paid their lawyers more than a million dollars in the subsequent litigations. A million dollars! I paused and told Peter, "It's not a million dollars. You are forgetting to deduct the thousand dollars you saved by not hiring me on the front end. So if you deduct what you saved, it is only $999,000 that you needlessly spent on lawyers these past several years."

Peter did not see the humor in that remark, and I have not seen him since. The moral of the story is to avoid do-it-yourself solutions. As noted above, the Internet has made it exceedingly easy to incorporate without a lawyer. Those systems however are only appropriate for the simplest routine aspects of the process. Anything beyond that requires legal counsel.

What mistake did Peter make (aside from not having legal counsel)? The choice of entity was actually correct (an LLC), but the structure was wrong. No one invests in hotels or other high-risk projects that have ongoing capital requirements without some sort of "out"—that is, an intermediate special purpose entity to shelter liability. Had they understood the nature of an LLC, they would have avoided getting a $999,000 lesson in its law.

Chapter 3

Capitalization

Capitalization is at the heart of new company formation. One of the more important issues that a new or start-up company must deal with relates to capital structure. What percentages will the various stakeholders own? How will earnings be distributed? How will the proceeds of a sale or other exit be split up? Will one stakeholder receive a share of sales proceeds ahead of any other? Will voting rights follow ownership percentages? What must parties contribute in exchange for their interests? All of these issues are initially defined in the company's capital structure.

a. Common Stock

ii. Founders' Stock

First of all, the receipt of stock is not nontaxable just because it is "founders' stock." Founders' stock refers to the common stock that is initially issued to the company's founders or organizers. The issuance of founders' stock is generally nontaxable either because its value is equal to the small amount of cash that the founders pay for it or because the founders contribute property for their stock under section 351 of the Internal Revenue Code.[13]

---

[13] Code section 351 provides that no gain or loss will be recognized if property is transferred to a corporation by one or more persons solely in exchange for stock in such corporation, and immediately after the exchange, such person or persons are in control (i.e., own 80 percent) of the corporation.

Some companies will add founders at some point after formation and will naturally assume that the new founders' shares can be received tax free since they received their shares tax free. This may or may not work, and a review of the tax rules is helpful to understanding why.

When a service provider (including a founder) buys stock in a corporation, the difference between what he pays for the stock and its value is taxable as compensation to the service provider. Most founders are service providers and, thus, will recognize income equal to the difference between cost and value on incorporation. However, upon formation, the founders may take the position that there is no difference since the value of the stock is equal to the small amount of cash that they contribute to cover formation costs. That probably works at the very beginning of a company's life; however, most companies will then move quickly to entering into supplier and customer contracts, building technology assets, contracting with employees and other service providers, and so forth. That activity creates value, specifically goodwill, which will cause the value of the stock to correspondingly increase. Thus, the tax-free issuance of founders' stock for nominal cash only works at the very early stages of the company's formation.

Suppose instead that the founders deferred the decision to incorporate until *after* they have created technology, hired contractors, and generally created value. Can they still incorporate tax free? The answer is yes, under section 351.

Generally, the exchange of assets for stock is a taxable transaction. Section 351 of the Internal Revenue Code provides for nonrecognition of taxable gain when a person or group of persons exchanges property for stock and, immediately after, the exchange owns more than 80 percent of the company's stock. In the typical case, the founders as a group will own 100 percent of the stock after the initial issuance, and thus meet the requirements of the statute. This does not work, however, when a founder comes along after the initial issuance and contributes property for stock, unless he or she (and others who are part of a plan) will own more than 80 percent after that issuance.

In addition, the founder must contribute property to the corporation in exchange for stock in order to obtain tax-free treatment. The term "property" is quite broadly defined to include legally protectable know-how and secret processes. A letter of intent, for example, has been held to be property in a related context[14] because the parties viewed it as having value. A grant of nonexclusive patent rights to a subsidiary was also held to be property.[15] "Broad" does not mean unlimited, however, and there comes a point where the rights granted do not rise to the level of property. In that case, they may be more service related. In other words, if the thing being contributed is so unripe as to not constitute "property," the stock received in return may be granted in anticipation and consideration of the taxable services that will be rendered to make it property.

Another tax trap lies in a transaction in which debt is assumed. If the debt assumed exceeds the value of the transferred assets or the transferor's basis in the transferred assets, the transaction will generally be taxable to some extent. A company can be incorporated tax free, but the fact that shares are being issued to founders does not necessarily make it so.

ii.   Vesting

It is generally a good idea for a founder to agree to vesting restrictions right up front, even though the founder might be the one that gets kicked out of the company and lose all of his or her unvested shares. For starters, an investor is likely to ask for a vesting restriction, and if one founder is difficult or unreasonable, that is just one more thing that must be negotiated later. Secondly, in my experience, any company that has more than four founders is highly likely to lose one or more of them in the first year. I cannot say why or give you any statistics, but I can say anecdotally that it is hard to get five people to share a common vision of a start-up for the first year.

---

[14] United States *v.* Stafford, 727 F.2d 1043 (11th Cir. 1984).
[15] E.I. DuPont de Nemours *v.* United States, 471 F.2d 1211 (Ct. Cl. 1973).

As the business matures and its model proves itself, parties may be increasingly willing to stick with it in the face of competing opportunities, divorces, changed circumstances, job changes, and so forth. Until then, the founders should plan on losing people, and when they do, they will want the departing persons' shares back so they can use that equity to replace the departees.

The tax rules with regard to unvested stock are harsh. Generally, stock that is subject to a substantial risk of forfeiture (i.e., nonvested) is treated as transferred to the owner when the restrictions lapse (i.e., as the shares vest). If the stock appreciates between the time of grant and date of vesting, it will be treated as having been transferred at a value higher than the price paid, which is a taxable event for the founder. Worse, because the founder will be an employee, it is an event that creates a withholding tax obligation for the company. The tax code allows a person to avoid this harsh result by electing to treat the issuance of nonvested shares as a transfer of the shares at the time of grant or issuance, rather than later when the shares vest. Thus, the compensation element in the transaction closes, and there is no further tax event when the shares vest. This election is referred to as a section 83(b) election. The section 83(b) election must be in writing, signed by the taxpayer, and filed within thirty days of the date of issuance—if it is one day late, it is wholly ineffective. In addition, the taxpayer must prove that it has been filed (by certified mail or having a file-stamped copy). The failure to file an 83(b) election is one of the most common mistakes a start-up company makes, and those involved usually pay for it at exit.

b. Options

An option is simply a right to buy a certain number of shares ("option shares") of stock at a certain price (the "exercise price" or "strike price"). Under current rules, the exercise price of an option must be the fair market value of the underlying option shares as of the date of grant of the option. Thus, if the value of the shares increases (as is expected), the option becomes more valuable ("in the money"), allowing the employee or optionee to "wait and see" before incurring a tax cost or realizing a financial benefit. If the stock value increases, the optionee will exercise and participate in that increase in value. If it decreases, the optionee will not exercise and not be out any money. There is a cost to that wait-and-see feature, as discussed below.

Securities and Corporate Law. An option is a security and thus must be granted in accordance with federal and state securities laws. Some states, such as California, require a securities notice to be filed with the state. No federal filings are required for private companies, but there are detailed rules on what must be in an option plan and what value of shares may be optioned.[16] Importantly, a written plan is required, and for federal purposes, options may be granted only to individuals in order to meet the requirements of applicable securities law registration exemptions.

Exercise Price. Current tax rules require an option to be granted at fair market value as of the date of grant (see the discussion on section 409A below). If an option is granted to an employee at less than fair market value, the employee is subject to taxes, penalties, and interest. The company also has withholding obligations. Because of the potentially large tax exposure, almost all venture-backed companies will obtain a professional valuation to support their option price, and all companies should.

More often, in a start-up company environment, problems arise in connection with a promise of an option grant at a certain price. An option is not granted until it is *formally* granted, meaning that necessary corporate action has been taken, so an

---

[16] Rule 701 of the Securities Act of 1933. Companies can offer their securities under a written compensatory plan without having to comply with federal securities registration requirements, if total sales of stock during a twelve-month period do not exceed the greater of $1 million, fifteen percent of the issuer's total assets, or fifteen percent of all the outstanding securities of that class.

offer letter promising to make a grant does not result in a completed grant that locks in the strike price. That price will be measured not at the date of the offer letter but at the date of grant, and anyone who has been reading the newspapers lately knows that no backdating is allowed.

Exercise Currency. Generally, my rule is that options should be reserved for the rank and file. While there are exceptions to my rule, C-level executives should hold stock instead of options if possible. First, higher-level persons should have "skin in the game," while an option is designed to be no risk (until exercise). Second, proceeds from a sale of stock may be taxed at lower capital gains rates than proceeds from cashing out an option. The problem with stock ownership, however, is that there is a cost to acquiring stock, whether in the form of an option exercise price, purchase price, or simply the taxes resulting from a compensatory grant of stock. Thus, the employee or optionee has a difficult choice—either (i) exercise an option and incur the out-of-pocket cost of paying the exercise price but obtain a potentially better tax result, or (ii) not exercise, not incur the cost of paying the exercise price, but be taxed at higher ordinary income tax rates.

A creative way around the problem is to allow an executive to buy his stock (or exercise his option) with a promissory note instead of cash—usually with a wink and nod understanding that the company will not ask for payment of the note if the stock decreases in value. The problem with that plan is that the decision to enforce the note may not be up to current management when the time comes and instead might be in the hands of a creditor or bankruptcy trustee. Thus, the clever executive will get the company to agree that the note will be wholly "nonrecourse." The term "nonrecourse" means that upon default, the company can take the shares back (subject to collection procedures imposed by law) but cannot hold the executive personally liable.

This works well as a corporate law matter in many states, but as a tax matter, the IRS does not view this arrangement as any different from an option and will tax the transaction as though it were an option. This means that the executive gets no holding period credit until he actually pays the note and also may have gain on each payment date when he is deemed to "own" the underlying shares. The compromise solution to this problem is to allow the employee to purchase his shares with a promissory note that has "limited recourse." By "limited recourse" I mean that the creditor (the company) would be limited in the amount of personal assets of the debtor that it could seize to satisfy payment of the note. For example, a fifty percent recourse note would mean that the debtor is only personally liable for half the amount of the note, and the creditor could sue and recover that limited amount from the debtor's personal assets. The amount of recourse required for the IRS to respect it as payment is not entirely clear, but 51 percent is generally assumed to be safe in a start-up company environment.[17] Of course, that means that the executive will eventually have to pay that amount regardless of what happens to the shares.

Incentive Stock Options (ISOs) vs. Nonstatutory Options (NSOs). Most stock plans allow for the grant of nonstatutory options and incentive stock options. The amount by which the value of the option shares exceeds the exercise price (the "spread") on an NSO is immediately taxable as ordinary income on exercise. The spread on an ISO, however, is not taxed until the option shares are sold, which is why ISOs are popular. However, the spread on an ISO is an adjustment to alternative minimum taxable income, which may result in alternative minimum tax so, except for relatively small grants, it is not quite accurate to view ISOs as tax free.[18] In addition, an option is only an ISO to the extent it is exercisable as to $100,000 worth of stock in any calendar year.

---

[17] The amount of recourse may be as low as 25 percent in a more mature company. This is a facts and circumstances test and there are no hard and fast guidelines.

[18] The gain on exercise of an ISO is an item of tax preference and will attract an alternative minimum tax when total preferences exceed applicable exemption amounts.

If the shares received on exercise of an ISO (the ISO shares) are held for at least one year from exercise and two years from grant, gain on sale of the shares will be taxed at capital gains rates. If the shares are disposed of before the expiration of those time periods, however, the transaction is referred to as a "disqualifying disposition" and the gain is taxed at ordinary rates.

Early Exercise. Options can vest, just like stock, or, to be more accurate, the underlying option shares can be made subject to a right of repurchase at cost that lapses over time based on continued employment. Options can be exercisable for vested shares in accordance with a vesting schedule or can be exercised for nonvested shares, which is known as "early exercise."

As noted above, the spread in an NSO is taxed at ordinary rates on exercise and any gain attributable to appreciation in the option stock after the exercise will be taxable at capital gains rates if the one-year holding period for long-term capital gains purposes is met. Because exercise closes the compensation element in the option, many employees are tempted to exercise their option early and exercise for nonvested shares if possible. This works fine for an NSO that later appreciates. If, however, the option shares decrease in value, the employee will be out of pocket for the exercise price of the option shares.

Many employees believe that they should always exercise early to start the holding period and lock in this favorable capital gains tax treatment. This is not always a great solution, as a lot of Silicon Valley executives discovered during the dot-com days of the late '90s. Here is why. An executive would exercise an option while it was in the money and its value seemed to be going higher. Sometimes, the exercise price and the "spread" would both be substantial, resulting in a large payment, as well as a large tax bill on exercise. Sometimes, the executive would pay for the stock with a promissory note and basically bet that he or she could pay the note with the proceeds of a later sale of the stock on exit. Then, the value of the stock would fall to an amount below the original exercise price, and the executive would sell the stock or claim a worthless stock deduction.

The problem, as many found out, was that the income on exercise was ordinary income, taxable immediately at high rates. The loss on the later sale was capital, deductible only against $3,000 per year of ordinary income plus capital gains. The result would be a large economic loss but very little tax deduction. I saw more than one executive whose tax liability—as a result of exercise—exceeded his or her net worth. As you can imagine, many employees have been surprised at how the tax law works in this scenario, but Silicon Valley executives do not engender much sympathy in Congress.

To put real numbers to it, suppose you have an NSO to acquire $1,000,000 worth of stock for an exercise price of $200,000. You exercise the option because you know the value of the stock is going to go higher and higher, and you want to lock in your ability to get capital gains on the excess. On exercise, you have $800,000 of gain and pay tax at 35 percent federal, plus state tax, if applicable. Then, the economy hits another recession, the stock drops to a value of $200,000, and the company is sold. You paid $200,000 for your shares, and you received $200,000 back. How much did you make?

You lost a little less than $280,000. How? Taxable gain on exercise: $800,000 times tax rate of 35 percent = $280,000. Deductible loss on sale: $3,000.

And if the stock had decreased even more, you would have lost that much more of the exercise price. Granted, the unused capital losses can be carried over and used to offset capital gains plus $3,000 per year of ordinary income, but at that rate, the present value of those losses is much less than the tax cost. Even if the taxpayer does have capital gains that can be reduced by the capital losses, the result is uneven because the income was taxed at 35% but the losses offset income that would be taxed at 15%. This is why exercise is often a risky strategy as a tax matter.

Options and Independent Contractors. Typically, an option expires upon the termination of employment of the optionee, since an objective of an option plan is to entice employees to stick around until exit. When an option is allowed to sit unexercised after an employee leaves, an "overhang" is created.[19] This overhang can wreak havoc with a capitalization table if it gets too large, since it makes it hard to determine the fully diluted capitalization of the company. For example, for purposes of valuing a company, an investor will assume that all options reserved under a plan will be exercised; however, everyone knows that employees will leave employment and let their options lapse unexercised so that they are returned to the pool and can be used for further grants. If a substantial amount of options will not expire until some date that is far out in the future, it is more difficult for an investor to anticipate how many shares will be outstanding on an exit.

With employees, the date of termination is not hard to determine. For independent contractors, however, it is not always clear when they have terminated service since their service may be only periodic. A well-advised company will clarify in writing when that termination has occurred, either by designating in the plan documents what events are deemed to be a termination of service or by expressly terminating service in writing.

Notice on Termination. As mentioned, options lapse automatically if not exercised within a certain period of time after termination of service. Formal notice of the fact that an option is about to lapse is generally not required to be given, until you talk to a litigator. Although no option plan will obligate an employer to notify an employee of an option lapse, the cautious company will, as a matter of course, notify terminated employees in advance—in writing—of the lapse of their options.

Magic Backdating Ink. Under current tax rules, options must be granted at fair market value, meaning that the exercise price of an option must be fair market value of the stock at the date of grant. For as long as I can remember, clients have asked me if they can "paper" an option grant that had been promised

---

[19] "Overhang" includes stock options granted, plus those reserved for grant, as a percentage of the total shares outstanding.

long before. I have always discouraged this practice, even for private companies. My reasoning was that even if no one cared about the accounting consequence (because the company was not publicly traded, for example), we did care about the tax consequences. ISOs must be granted at fair market value, and even NSOs should not be granted with an exercise price far below value ("deep in the money") or they could be "deemed exercised" by the IRS, resulting in immediate taxation. Moreover, the documents simply would not accurately reflect the facts or be consistent with the stock plan, which provided for an exercise price determined at grant.

Notwithstanding the issues with backdating options, the practice was widespread for private companies prior to 2002. Public companies were another story since option grant dates were significant for accounting and reporting purposes, at least theoretically.

So imagine my surprise when I read about one stock-option-backdating case after another. As of this writing, Silicon Valley executives have been criminally convicted for making it falsely appear that options had been granted at a lower price on an earlier date.

Here is how it works. Suppose the CEO tells you on Friday that he is going to recommend that your company grant you a stock option. The stock is trading at twenty dollars on Friday. On the following Monday, the board approves the stock option grant, but the value has gone up to twenty-two dollars by then. Now your option price has increased to twenty-two dollars and you have to pay an extra two dollars per share to exercise. "Can't we just pretend that it was issued last Friday?" you might ask, since that is when it was promised. In fact, as long as we are pretending, why can't we pretend that it was issued last Tuesday, when the price was eighteen dollars? And thus we start sliding down the slippery backdating slope. A 2000 e-mail among officials at one Silicon Valley tech company referred to this ability to backdate or leave dates open while we wait and see as "magic backdating ink."[20]

As a tax and accounting matter, "backdating" results in the optionee paying less than fair market value at grant to exercise.

---

[20] *See* Options lawsuit gives up details / Shareholders suing Mercury Interactive over timing of grants, SF Gate February 21, 2007.

In other words, if the stock is worth more than the exercise price on the actual date of grant than on the "pretend" date of grant, the optionee will have paid less than fair market value for the stock. If the company does not record that expense because it is clinging to the fiction of a grant when the stock was worth less, its financial statements will not accurately reflect the size of the stock option expense. Thus, income will be overstated and the investors will have been given false financial information.

In the private company world, we may not be concerned about what the accountants think about inaccurately dated option grants, since private companies may not provide anyone with financial statements. Even for private companies, however, one constituency does care about grant dates, and that is the IRS. Under current law, even NSOs must be granted to employees at fair market value, or the employee will have immediate income, penalties, and interest.[21] The days of private company option backdating are over.

Summary. Options are a great tool for rewarding employees and service providers; however, they are fraught with potential problems for the company that is not well advised. My top ten most frequent option problems to watch for are as follows:

1. No professional valuation, resulting in potential taxes and penalties

2. No written plan or grant documents

3. Backdated grant documents

4. Lack of 83(b) elections on early exercises

5. ISO exercises resulting in alternative minimum tax

6. Grants to non-individuals

7. Lack of securities law filings or compliance

---

[21] *See* IRC section 409A.

8.   Excessive overhang

9.   Extended exercise periods

10. Large grants to high-level employees

c.   Preferred Stock

Preferred stock is what your company will sell to investors to raise money. The stock is called "preferred" because it has some sort of liquidation and dividend preference, meaning that on sale of the company, the preferred stockholders will be paid before the common stockholders, and if there is not enough money to pay everyone, the preferred stockholders will take all the proceeds. The amount of this "liquidation preference" is negotiated and may be participating or nonparticipating. Participating preferred stock gets its money back *and* then shares in sales proceeds based on its percentage ownership. Nonparticipating preferred stock only gets its money back (or a multiple of its money) and does not share in the upside beyond that. Preferred stock is also usually convertible into common stock at some agreed-upon ratio (usually 1:1) so that nonparticipating preferred stock will convert if the percentage of the company allocable to a share of stock exceeds its liquidation preference. Investors will also negotiate a host of other protective provisions.

Although preferred stock has rights that the common stock does not, there are good reasons that the common stockholders would want the company to issue preferred stock instead of common stock to investors. From the company's standpoint, it receives more dollars for each share than it would receive from the sale of an equal amount of common stock. The investor will be happy because it is protected on the downside by its liquidation preferences.

Preferred stock is not always the answer. Sometimes, other types of securities make more sense. Mistakes around preferred stock come in two varieties—companies issue it when they should not or do not issue it when they should.

When a Company Should Not Issue Preferred Stock but Does. The sale of preferred stock necessarily requires a company to value its stock. When dealing with institutional or sophisticated investors who are investing enough money to justify extensive due diligence, that valuation is not hard to justify. With smaller numbers, however, the compliance costs might discourage arriving at an accurate valuation. If, as a result, the company is valued too high, the next round will be a "down round," possibly requiring "antidilution adjustments" that further reduce the founders' percentage interests. If the value is too low, the founders will have given up too much in the first preferred stock round and will lose control that much more quickly. My rule of thumb is that if a company cannot raise at least $1 million in its financing round, I do not (as company counsel) recommend the use of preferred stock. Does that mean the company should sell common stock to raise money? Absolutely not, for the reasons discussed below.

When a Company Should Issue Preferred Stock but Does Not. The flip side of the company that is too early to issue preferred stock is the company that should sell preferred stock but instead sells common stock. If there is only one thing in this chapter that you should remember, it is that you never sell common stock to raise money. Common stock is to be used to issue to founders, issue on exercise of options, or sell to C-level executives. In other words, common stock must be cheap. If the value of the common stock is too high, the option price must be high, and the company's options (which must have a fair-market-value exercise price) will not be attractive to optionees. Selling common stock for cash will necessarily result in a higher common stock price. If it does not, that will mean that the common stock is being priced too cheap, and the founders are giving up too much of the company for the initial sale of stock.

So if a company that needs less than $1 million cannot sell preferred stock or common stock, what can it do? The answer is convertible debt.

d. Warrants and Convertibles

Convertible debt (or debt with warrants) solves the problem of the company's current need for cash when it is not in a position to sell preferred stock. As noted above, the investor in a note gets the security of debt (which must be repaid before the equity gets a return) and need not gamble on a valuation. The company gets its investment without having to set a valuation. Both parties avoid a long and costly negotiation of equity terms.

Often the debt is secured and carries a higher-than-average interest rate. Since many technology companies do not have much in the way of hard assets to offer as security, the debt holder is really taking an equity risk, despite the security interest it might take in "technology." To reward the debt holder for investing early (before the company's larger preferred stock round), the debt holder will be allowed to convert at a discount or will be given "warrant coverage."

The discount means that the debt will convert at a lower price than the preferred stock price. A typical discount can range from ten to thirty percent depending on market conditions and the particular company. For example, a twenty percent discount would mean that each eighty dollars of debt would convert into one hundred dollars' worth of preferred stock when the company does its financing. Alternatively, the investor could have warrant coverage. Twenty percent warrant coverage, for example, typically would mean that (in addition to converting its debt) the investor would have the right to buy twenty dollars' worth of preferred stock for each one hundred dollars of debt that it holds.[22] If the warrant strike price is nominal (one cent per share, for example), warrant coverage could be similar to discount, with more paperwork. Sometimes, investors get both.

Over the last few years, more and more convertible debt instruments have included a price cap. Many investors have had

---

[22] Warrant coverage is sometimes calculated off a number other than the principal amount of the note or other debt instrument.

the unpleasant experience of investing in a company's convertible debt, and then watching the company use its investment dollars to increase its value, which of course increases the price per share at which their debt would convert. In a sense, the terms of traditional convertible debt place the debt holders and the company at cross purposes—the debt holders would like a low valuation at the equity financing stage while the company seeks to maximize value.

In fact, there are stories in the Silicon Valley of debt holders talking later investors out of investing at high values because of the potential dilution they would suffer. The perceived answer to the debt holder's dilemma is a price cap. A "cap" means that the debt will convert at the lesser of a discount to the price offered in the next equity financing or a price per share determined as if the company were worth $X. In that scenario, X is some reasonable estimate of the value at the next financing. (In practice, the cap is actually a bit higher than the expected valuation, since it is a downside protection device and not intended to be a valuation trigger.)

Similarly, the sophisticated investor will ask that in the event of a sale before a financing, they receive an equity return. In other words, upon a sale of the company, unless the debt has converted, the investor will receive some multiple of the investment.

There are a couple of traps in this. First, the discount should be "market" and not more than that. Market may depend on how hard it is for the company to raise money. As stated, twenty percent is common, but it could be much higher if the company has no other options. Second, whatever the discount, it is coming out of the founders' hides and not the Series A investors'. While it might seem like the eventual Series A investors are being forced to carve out a piece of what they are getting at a cheap price, in fact, the Series A investors will take the effect of debt conversion into account to ensure that they end up with whatever percent of the company they desire. In other words, regardless of the size of the discount to the debt holders, the later investor will decide what percent of the company it needs for its investment, and it will simply price the preferred stock at whatever price it takes to get to that result.

Finally—and this is a big trap—an S corporation is limited in its ability to issue convertible debt. As noted earlier, an S corporation can only have one class of stock and will often issue convertible debt in order to avoid having to issue preferred stock (the issuance of which would terminate its S election). That all works fine unless the debt converts to common stock at a discount, because if the debt is not convertible at fair market value, it may be treated as stock. If the convertible debt holder is not a US individual, and the debt is treated as stock for tax purposes, the corporation may be treated as having a disqualified shareholder. And finally, even if the debt is convertible to common stock and is held by a US individual, the debt might be treated as stock that does not share in distributions, thus creating the prohibited second class of stock. This is tricky stuff and requires counsel from someone who understands S corporations. Losing an S election is an expensive mistake to make.

e.   Phantom Stock, SARs, and Virtual Stock

The Silicon Valley was built on equity compensation (stock for sweat). For many years, we had it pretty good out on the West Coast—options could be granted at artificially low prices, and so long as the value was not too far off, the regulators accepted the board's good-faith determination of value. No more! Code section 409A requires a company to be correct in its option valuation, and if it is wrong, the results are draconian—taxes and penalties approaching the value of the option grant (when state taxes and penalties are included). Since the only way to know for sure that you are right in valuation is to obtain an expensive valuation, many companies are rethinking the value of an option plan.

The problem is exacerbated in the case of an S corporation, since the exercise of an option on S corporation stock could result in a loss of the S election if the optionee is not a qualified S corporation shareholder. LLCs do not have that problem, but they have other issues. In particular, the exercise of an option on an LLC interest requires complicated accounting entries that, as a practical matter, most companies will not bother with or understand. The exercising optionee of an LLC option will be a member and receive the IRS Form 1065, Schedule K-1, which will require the optionee to pay tax on the income of the LLC, whether he or she receives it or not. That may not be the great result everyone intended.

For those reasons, S corporations and LLCs have long used phantom stock (instead of real stock, options, or LLC interests) to reward and motivate employees. Here is how it works. The company promises to reserve a portion of the proceeds of a sale or exit "off the top" for distribution to holders of phantom stock units. That amount, whatever it is, is then divided by the number of units in the plan. Each holder of a unit then shares in the proceeds of the sale based on his or her relative number of units. Those units can be made subject to vesting or can be granted in tranches. The only catch is that the unit holder must be employed at the date of the liquidity event (like a sale of the company). In this way, a phantom unit mimics an option in a privately held company.

Options are often cashed out at exit (and not exercised) and expire if not exercised within a short period of time after termination of employment. Most options on private company stock expire unexercised, meaning that typically the only employees who cash out of options are those who are employed when the liquidity event happens. Of course, unlike a phantom plan unit holder, an option holder has the ability to terminate employment, exercise the option, and hold the stock until a sale of the company, and that does happen sometimes.

The downside is that the phantom units are not stock—even though they are stock-like—so holders do not vote or otherwise share in current earnings, although they could be drafted to share in current distributions and often are. Phantom units typically expire if the employee leaves before an exit, unlike stock. Most significantly, there is no possibility for capital gains tax treatment with a phantom unit. It is compensation, taxed at the highest federal and state rates (plus payroll taxes). An option, as well as a grant of stock or membership interests, can potentially qualify for low capital gains tax rates.

The benefit of the phantom stock plan is simplicity. In fact, it is so simple that there are really only a few ways that a company could screw it up. One is to not think through how proceeds are divvied up on exit. Importantly, the proceeds to be divided must be proceeds *net* of liabilities. So, if a company ends up getting sold for liability assumption, and there is nothing left over for the shareholders, there should also be nothing for the optionees. Always split net.

Second, the amount to be divided should be based on the total number of units reserved under the plan, not the total issued. For example, if the company reserves ten percent of the net proceeds of a sale for distribution under the plan, and if there is only one unit holder at the time of the exit—and he has been granted ten percent of the units in the plan—he should get one percent and not ten percent of the net proceeds of the sale. Sounds simple, but companies regularly get this wrong because they assume that they will eventually issue all the units but then fail to do so.

Finally, it is pretty easy to inadvertently end up within the penalty provisions of Code section 409A. The easiest way for management to run afoul of section 409A is to allow unit holders to keep their units long after departing, which converts the plan into a deferred compensation plan under 409A. If the plan then does not comply with 409A, the result will be a tax disaster.

There are some traps, but if it is well structured, a phantom plan is a simple, cost-effective, and elegant equity compensation vehicle. Poorly planned, it can be a disaster.

Chapter 4

Employment Law Issues

Companies, even start-up companies, are not people and by definition can only act through the people that they hire. Thus, no company will avoid employment law issues. Misinformation abounds in the employment area, and if you are unlucky enough to be an employer in a state like California, you will soon receive an education in the laws that protect employees and impose obligations on employers. Employment law problems can be broken down into two broad categories: employers' obligations to employees and employees' obligations to previous employers. In either case, a start-up company needs to care for each.

a.   Classification

Employees are expensive. The employer must withhold taxes from its income and report and pay over those amounts on a regular basis. The taxes that must be accounted for include federal, state, and local income taxes, FICA, FUTA, and state disability, to name a few. Federal and state unemployment insurance contributions cannot be forgotten, and then there is the matter of workers' compensation insurance. The collection and reporting obligation is daunting, so much so that it is a rare founder that will get this right without some trial and error.

Because of the enormous hassle and expense of having employees, it is usually not long before someone comes up with the bright idea that he or she will not hire employees. Instead, this person will only hire independent contractors. In fact, even the officers will be independent contractors. Then there is no need to worry about any of this stuff, right?

Misclassification issues are easily the lowest-hanging fruit the Internal Revenue Service can go after if it takes an interest in a start-up company. From the viewpoint of the federal and state tax collectors, the title given the individual service provider is not determinative of his or her true status as an employee or independent contractor.

To make that determination, the IRS has a twenty-factor test—although in reality, it boils down to who has the right of direction and control. Is the individual given a project and told to come back with a certain result or product? Or is he or she subject to the direction and control of the employer? While there is a certain amount of structuring that can be done around these rules, for the most part, a company may be required to retain the prohibited direction and control as a business matter. In particular, officers are by definition subject to the direction and control of the board and will always be employees— notwithstanding the risky notion that there can be contractor CEOs.

So what happens if a company gets it wrong, and it pays a person as an independent contractor and does not withhold as an employee? Whose problem is it anyway?

The IRS imposes a 100 percent penalty on the employer based on underwithheld amounts. However, as a practice, it only collects it once. What this means is that the IRS can go directly to the employer if the employee does not pay the taxes on the compensation he or she received from the employer. You can assume that the IRS will always do that. In fact, the way the issue may come up is that some clever employees will "turn themselves in" to the IRS and ask the IRS to go back after the employer for underwithheld taxes. That way, the employees get their taxes paid, and the employer ends up paying them. After adding penalties and interest, the cost of failing to withhold due to misclassification can be very high.

So, does the start-up company take its best shot at withholding? That is better than not trying at all, but there is a better answer. There are payroll services that do this for a living, and you can generally be assured that tax withholding is being properly handled when such a service is engaged. Granted, it is not cheap, but it is one area that is best outsourced, at least until the company can hire a dedicated human resources person to monitor payroll tax compliance.

How about if the company doesn't pay its people or just pays them in stock? Does that help solve the problem? In fact, the nature of "sweat equity" is that the founders (i.e., employees) work for stock and not cash. There is no withholding on that stock because it is sold or granted early in the company's life at a nominal value. Problem solved? Not in California, at least.

b. State Minimum Wage and Hour Laws

In a huge disconnect between law and reality, federal and state minimum wage laws require even start-up company employees to receive at least the minimum wage. In the real world, start-up companies do not have the cash to pay any wages, not even minimum wage, and even if they did, the collection of nondeductible capital contributions from the founders—to be immediately repaid as taxable wages—would not be very efficient. The only good news is that the market does not seem to penalize start-up companies much for failing to pay minimum wage, even though a founder who gets booted out of the company may have an unpaid wage claim against the company. The safe course is to bite the bullet and actually pay minimum wages, as inefficient and nonsensical as that might seem to businesspersons.

c. Deferred Compensation

Many start-up companies take the approach that they will "defer" their founders' salaries until a funding event. That way, they reason, they comply with wage laws and are not paying themselves with their own nondeductible contributions. This issue usually first surfaces when the company is asked (by an investor) to produce a balance sheet, and noted under current liabilities will be a line item for deferred salaries. Instead of "deferred salaries," the item should more properly read, "deferred but never-to-be-paid salaries," because that is a likely result.

Under some state laws, such as California's, employees must receive payment at least semimonthly. Even if a company is willing to take the minimum-wage-law risk (and almost all of them are), an institutional investor is not going to be crazy about allowing his or her investment to go into the company and then right back out of the company into the founders' pockets as deferred salary. After all, that is what they got their stock for. Nevertheless, for the right companies, this sometimes happened, but that was before Code section 409A.

Code section 409A has been mentioned a couple of times now. Section 409A basically imposes strict rules on the manner, time, and form of payment of deferred compensation. Although 409A was enacted to combat deferred compensation abuses that were dreamt up on the compensation committees of large public corporations, its scope is so much broader than that. Given a broad grant of authority from Congress, the Internal Revenue Service has applied section 409A in counterintuitive and counterproductive ways to situations that have no potential for abuse. It has also collected a lot of tax by doing so.

The 409A problem with deferring founders' salaries is that 409A requires that an election to defer compensation be in place by December 31 of the year prior to the year in which the compensation is earned. The arrangement must also specify when the compensation will be paid and the payment may not be improperly accelerated.[23] Because of their complexity, many salary deferral plans will fail to comply with the 409A rules.

Unlike accepting some state labor law risk for violating minimum wage laws, the tax effect of violating 409A is neither merely a matter of risk nor a cost that a company can justify. If 409A is violated, the penalties are taxation of vested amounts—a twenty percent additional tax and interest at the IRS "late payment" rate plus one percent. In addition, some "Code-conformity" states, such as California, will also impose tax and an identical 20 percent penalty, resulting in a tax that eats up most of the value of the payment—not a cost that can be easily justified.

d. Sexual Harassment, Discrimination, and Related Claims

My former client, Gary, was the founder of a successful company that published web content. The company started out as a mom-and-pop business, with just Gary and his wife handling all aspects of the business. The company soon grew into a larger business with numerous staff and an independent board of directors. Gary took his corporate responsibilities seriously, and the board met regularly to approve certain actions and oversee the business. He consulted his lawyers (including me) often, and from all outward appearances, he seemed to be doing everything right.

Gary's background was as a writer, and despite his increased role in management, Gary continued to write all the content for the company's site. He was an older guy, close to sixty years old, and he seemed to have finally honed his craft and was realizing

---

[23] Distributions under a nonqualified deferred compensation plan can only be payable upon the employee's separation from service, disability, death, a fixed time or schedule specified under the plan, a change in ownership or control of the corporation or a substantial portion of the assets of the corporation, or the occurrence of an unforeseeable emergency.

the benefits of his efforts. One afternoon, Gary showed up at our office to tell me about a potential offer for the sale of his business. Gary excitedly told me that the sale price would allow him and his wife to finally move out of the "pillbox" that they lived in and into a bigger house in a better part of town.

Gary was an expressive guy. In fact, he was in the business of communication and was not really able to keep a secret from his employees, especially one employee in particular. Everything was going smoothly, discussions were moving ahead, and I even managed to finally get Gary to do some estate planning now that it looked like he would have substantial wealth soon. And then, a bomb was dropped on the company.

Not a real bomb, of course, but it had the same effect as a real bomb. This bomb came in the form of a letter from a lawyer, addressed and delivered to each and every member of the company's board, including Gary's wife. The letter had exhibits and attachments and went into great detail in pointing out relevant passages from the attachments. The letter was written on behalf of a young female staffer who had been working closely with Gary during the past year, but apparently not closely enough for Gary. She had accompanied Gary on business trips and in many after-hours evening meetings. In case you have not yet figured out where this is going, Gary was being accused of sexual harassment.

Often in these cases, a sexual harassment claim is a matter of "he said, she said." Unfortunately for Gary, the "he said" part was all in writing because Gary was an excellent writer. That was how he communicated. And in this case, that was how he engaged in his harassing conduct—in writing, in detail, and always very well written.

The e-mails and letters attached to the lawyer's letter told a story that was funny and sad, but most of all, graphic and obviously unwelcome. It recited Gary's, shall we say, preferences. It mentioned the woman's perceived physical shortcomings and Gary's generous willingness to overlook them. It recited the events of their meetings and trips and the resistance of the female staffer. It was poisonous, definitive, and incontrovertible. Beyond that, the thing that made it a company-ending event was Gary's insistence on clinging to an "it-doesn't-hurt-to-ask" defense, which, by the way, is not a good defense to this type of claim.

I wish I had a happy ending to this story. I wish I could say that the potential buyers were not spooked by the prospect of buying a lawsuit. I wish I could say that they settled on great terms and Gary's wife overlooked the whole thing with a "boys-will-be-boys" attitude. Unfortunately, that is not how things work in the real world. A sexual harassment claim, especially one that is well documented, can generate huge losses for a company.

That was ten years ago. Gary still lives in that "pillbox." His company limps along with just him now at the helm. The damage award did not leave room for expansion funds and, of course, derailed any possibility of a sale at a time when it was actually worth something.

e.   Your Employees Look Marvell-ous

Virginia Wei, senior director of business and legal affairs for Jasmine Networks, had her hands full. She was involved in negotiations regarding a sale of technology to one of Jasmine's competitors, Marvell Semiconductor. Jasmine was smaller than Marvell and privately held. Marvell was publicly traded and a much bigger and better-known company in the Silicon Valley.

Jasmine and Marvell were in the business of the design and manufacture of telecommunications chips, and technology was very important to their businesses. Thus, Jasmine was very careful to negotiate a nondisclosure agreement (NDA) with Marvell and to redact sensitive information. With respect to technical information, the parties agreed that Marvell could review but not copy information. The idea was to disclose enough information to demonstrate value but not so much as to disclose the secret. In particular, Jasmine blacked out the names and compensation information regarding the employee group that would go along with the technology if the sale closed.

Jasmine and Marvell agreed that Marvell would not conduct meetings with Jasmine's engineers without a representative of Jasmine present. To the uninitiated, it might have looked like Jasmine was being paranoid. After all, Marvell was a public company with a full staff of in-house attorneys. As it turned out, Jasmine's paranoia was well founded.

Wei returned to her office one day to find an innocuous message on her voice mail from the vice president and general counsel for Marvell. After leaving identification information, the Marvell team members concluded the call—or so they thought. Unfortunately, and ironically, this telecommunications company had not quite figured out how to hang up a phone at the end of a call, and Wei's voice mail continued to record the ensuing conversation. The group at Marvell then went on to discuss what would happen if they took Jasmine's intellectual property on the pretense of evaluating it and the possible repercussions should they be found out.

The reported court cases stated that, upon hearing the message of this conversation, Wei investigated whether Marvell had taken any action to obtain Jasmine's trade secrets. My guess is that it was a bit more dramatic than that. Wei probably went running down the hall to see how much damage had been done. She discovered that quite a lot had been disclosed. In particular, one of Jasmine's senior managers had secretly e-mailed Marvell stock option and salary information for Jasmine's engineers after Jasmine refused to provide that information. I am sure you can guess what happened next—a lot of litigators made a lot of money.

There is a moral in that story—several, in fact. I cannot say that Jasmine did anything wrong, but just imagine what would have happened if Marvell had known how to operate a speakerphone. Fortunately, Jasmine was lawyered up and had a solid NDA in place. It's not their fault if people did not abide by it—all the paper in the world cannot protect against that. And that is the moral of this story. Your agreements are only as good as the people who stand behind them. You cannot assume that a public company will act honestly, notwithstanding Sarbanes-Oxley, their code of conduct, or their "tone at the top." Those are platitudes thought up by academics and government officials who may or may not know what people are really like in business but are, in any event, ineffectual when it comes to regulating their conduct. Always assume that the guys on the other side of the deal are out to get you ... because they *are*.

f.   Over "Hurd" in the Boardroom

You gotta' love Mark Hurd. One little scandal has provided so much material—do not mix business and personal expenses, do not sexually harass, do not give ex-*Playboy* models the excuse to claim harassment, and above all, do not announce how you are going to kick your previous employer's ass when you get hired by its competitor.

For historical background, Mark Hurd was basically forced to resign after allegations that he falsified expense accounts. The allegations were made by a former HP consultant. In this age of transparency and heightened ethical standards, HP's board felt it best that Hurd leave HP, thus giving a competitor a reason to criticize the judgment of HP's board and an opportunity to hire Hurd.

That might be the end of the story, *but* Mr. Hurd, on exit, signed a settlement agreement that acknowledged his previous confidentiality obligations and agreed that he would not engage in conflicting business obligations that resulted in his unauthorized use or disclosure of HP's confidential information. Mr. Hurd received millions of dollars' worth of stock as severance and so, when he then accepted employment with Oracle, a direct competitor, HP sued to enjoin him from taking a position that would necessarily result in the disclosure of confidential trade secrets, such as information regarding HP's customers in the competing space.

The case quickly settled—Mr. Hurd surrendered his options, and HP dropped the suit, but the instructive part about all of this is more what HP did *not* say than what it did say. The HP lawsuit hammered on the potential disclosure of confidential and trade secret information and all the trouble HP had gone through to keep it top secret. It did *not* state that Hurd had agreed to a noncompete because, in California and many other states, a noncompete is unenforceable except in connection with the sale of the goodwill of a business. California courts, in fact, have been known to view the attempt to enforce an unenforceable noncompete against a departed employee as a violation of its unfair trade practices law, so it is inadvisable to use such clauses even for their *in terrorem* effect. Similarly, the nonhire and nonsolicitation clauses in Hurd's agreements referred to uses, solicitations, and communications that were made with the unauthorized assistance of HP's confidential information.

Surprisingly, a lot of lawyers miss this subtlety, and you will see many agreements that contain absolute no-hire or no-solicit clauses. What might have happened if HP had taken that sort of position? We need not guess because that is exactly what Arthur Andersen LLP did.

Raymond Edwards worked as a CPA for Arthur Andersen. When Edwards left, Andersen required him to sign a noncompetition agreement that, for a period of eighteen months, prohibited him from performing accounting services, soliciting clients, and soliciting any professional personnel from Andersen. It was not surprising that the noncompetition and nonsolicitation clauses were held to be illegal under California law, but more notably those clauses were held to be void and unenforceable as an unnecessary restraint on trade.[24] Other California cases have allowed employees to sue their employers for enforcing such provisions.[25] Rare is the occasion that someone can get in trouble by trying to enforce a business agreement, but this is

---

[24] Edwards *v.* Arthur Andersen LLP, 44 Cal.4th 937 (2008).
[25] Application Group, Inc. *v.* Hunter Group, Inc., 61 Cal. App. 4th 881 (Cal. Ct. App. 1998); Walia *v.* Aetna, Inc., 113 Cal. Rptr. 2d 737 (Cal. Ct. App. 2001) remanded 132 Cal.Rptr.2d 712, 66 P.3d 717 (2003).

one of those circumstances. So, to answer the question, had HP screwed up its agreements like Andersen did, and many companies still do, I expect that Mr. Hurd may have dared HP to try to enforce its agreements and kept his estimated $14 million of severance benefits. The moral of the story is to carefully draft and selectively enforce employee proprietary information agreements.

Chapter 5

Intellectual Property Protection

a.   Patents

Technology is one of the three legs of the Success Triangle (people, money, and technology). Most of the start-up companies in the Silicon Valley are based on their superior technology, and the first question a sophisticated investor will ask is, "Do you have patents?" You may not necessarily need patents to have technology, but you do need something that nobody else has and a way to keep them from getting it (at least without paying you).

Intellectual property rights include legally enforceable rights to keep another player from using a particular technology. For example, a patent might describe a method for building a computer chip, but its value is not in allowing someone to know how to build that exact same chip—it is in keeping that person from using your design and know-how in building that exact same chip. A start-up company may have technology (the know-how), but it must also have the right to keep others from using its technology.

A "patent" is an exclusive right granted by the US Patent and Trademark Office to an inventor or his or her assignee for a limited period of time in exchange for a public disclosure of an invention. A patent is not a right to use the invention; it is a right to exclude others from making, using, selling, offering for sale, or importing the patented invention for the term of the patent. Like any other property right, it may be sold, licensed, mortgaged, assigned or transferred, given away, or simply abandoned.

First, technology-oriented start-up companies should develop a sound strategy for protecting their intellectual capital as early as possible. For example, start-up companies sometimes start patenting without thinking through their long-term intellectual property management strategy. A common problem is a portfolio that is driven purely by research. A good intellectual property portfolio should be designed in a way that accurately covers the business objectives of the company while protecting the technologies around which the company is built and exploiting niches of the technology field that are not yet patented.

Second, intellectual property is thought of as a property right and can be sold and assigned like any other property right. Thus, the language of intellectual property rights transfers will be very similar to the language used in transferring tangible property. This similarity sometimes confuses people into thinking that the intellectual property is the technology or physical components in which it is embodied. This sort of thought might be okay in the workplace but falls apart in legal documents. For example, in a technology transfer transaction, a businessperson might state that he is selling a piece of equipment when what he means as a legal matter is that he is selling the technology that went into the creation of the equipment or, more accurately, the intellectual property rights that allowed the seller to prevent anyone else from producing that particular piece of equipment. The terminology will be important when enforcing the acquired rights.

Third, intellectual property rights must be assigned to the company. Before a company is fundable, the company must have clear ownership of its intellectual property, which means that the persons who have rights to the intellectual property must actually have assigned it. An agreement to assign is not the same as an assignment, and while the difference is subtle, it is significant. The case of Mark Holodniy provides a jarring example of the difference.

Mark Holodniy was a researcher for Stanford University, with whom he signed an agreement "agree[ing] to assign or confirm in writing to Stanford" his inventions. He then signed an agreement with Cetus Corporation, later purchased by Roche, stating that he "will assign and do[es] hereby assign to CETUS" rights and title to the inventions created while using Cetus's facilities. Stanford thereafter patented inventions that Holodniy helped create and sued Roche for patent infringement. The US Court of Appeals for the Federal Circuit dismissed Stanford's infringement claim because the agreement Holodniy signed with Cetus made Cetus—and later, Roche—the prior assignee of Holodniy's interest in the patents.[26]

The *Holodniy* case illustrates the importance of the exact words used in the assignment language. The implication is that "will assign" is different than "hereby assigns" and the ownership of the IP may turn on these small differences in language.

Who exactly has the intellectual property rights? In the case of patents, anyone who contributes to the invention may have a claim to the entire patent that covers the invention. This can arise casually or inadvertently, since oftentimes, founders will work on technology prior to the formation of a company with little or no formality. When the value of a company depends on the value of its intellectual property, which in turn depends on the ability to keep competitors out of the market, getting an assignment will be important.

What if the technology is not patented? Is it still worth anything? An invention can be legally protectable as a trade secret, and as a matter of cost, a company might decide to rely on trade secret protection. That is not a great strategy, as a patent registration could appear at any time, effectively putting them out of business. In the case of technology that is not patentable, how-

---

[26]Board of Trustees of the Leland Stanford Junior University *v.* Roche Molecular Systems, Inc., 583 F.3d 832, (Fed. Cir. 2009).

ever, trade secret protection may be all that is available. In that case, the value of the technology will lie in the owner's ability to enforce its rights under state law. Under state law, the trade secret must generally be valuable and, importantly, must be "secret," meaning that the owner has taken steps to preserve its confidentiality. Those steps usually require developing a trade secret protection policy and following it.

So, against that backdrop, here are the biggest IP blunders that start-up companies make:

1. Inadvertent Joint Ownership. As mentioned above, a founder that does not get an agreement with his collaborators is a joint owner. As a joint owner, the collaborator has the right to exploit the technology and IP individually, which of course destroys the ability of the founder to assign exclusive rights to a new company to be funded.

2. Failure to Assign. Closely related to the first item is the failure to get an assignment from those who have worked on the technology. It may seem like an easy matter to get the assignment later when there is a financier in place, but people disappear, attitudes change, and alliances evolve. The assignment should be in place from Day One.

3. Improperly Defined Rights. As mentioned above, the concept of IP ownership is a bit abstract, and agreements sometimes improperly describe certain tangible items rather than the underlying rights. Sometimes, even agreements that adequately define the rights being assigned do not go a step further and specify just who is going to do what to develop those rights.

4. No Strategy. As mentioned above, the people who write the patents tend to be technical people, not businesspeople, and as a result, the patents are necessarily research driven. Patents should be written with the current and future business in mind.

b. Trademark

Let me offer a few words about trademarks and trade names. Initially, a trademark is a distinctive mark used by someone to identify that his or her products or services are unique and to distinguish his or her products or services from those of others. A trademark is a type of intellectual property and can include a name, word, phrase, logo, symbol, design, or image.

A person acquires rights to a mark by using it, even without a federal registration. Eventually, that mark (and name) may become so associated with the company and its products as to be a large part of the company's goodwill. In fact, when a technology company is sold, it usually has very little on its balance sheet in hard assets—it is selling intangibles, such as intellectual property and goodwill. If that name and/or logo should be challenged or diluted, a large part of its goodwill might disappear.

The owner of a registered trademark can sue for infringement to prevent unauthorized use of his or her mark. Registration is not required, but an unregistered mark may be protectable only within the geographical area within which it has been used or in geographical areas into which it may be reasonably expected to expand. Thus, a competitor could exclude a company from using an unregistered mark in future markets.

In order to obtain federal registration, the mark must not be merely descriptive. In addition, even after a registration, the owner will not prevail on an infringement claim under the fair use doctrine if the alleged infringer can show that he is using the mark to describe accurately an aspect of its products. Thus, a name that is merely descriptive of a company's products (and its competitors' products) may not be a great choice for a mark. The issue is important to resolve early in the company's life since a large part of its future goodwill may be tied up in the mark, and the company or its acquirer would not want it to be subject to challenge at that time.

Chapter 6

Start-Up Capital Funding

Start-up companies are risky propositions. This may be one of the reasons that so many start-ups are run by millennials—they have the ability to swing for the fences and take big risks on new ideas. The rest of us have mortgages, alimony, whatever. The flip side to having nothing to lose is having nothing to invest—and that is why financing will loom large in the start-up company's plans. In fact, the first question that I ask when I meet a new start-up is, "Are you fundable?"

The question of "are you fundable?" is important to me since I take so many start-up companies on "spec" (i.e., I only get paid if they are successful, and relatively few are successful). Over the years, I have developed a system for deciding who is likely to be fundable and who is not. Granted, my system is not foolproof, but it is a system, and it relies on the Success Triangle described earlier.

The Success Triangle is comprised of great people, great technology, and money. If the first two factors are present, theoretically, the third will follow. This chapter describes the non-technical evaluation of people and technology.

1.   If It Sounds Like BS …

I learned this from an IP lawyer named Anne, who I worked for when I was a young associate. We were sitting in a conference room being interviewed by phone to act as counsel for a new start-up. The founder was trying to explain the technology and the business. Anne might not have been an engineer, but she had seen enough technology law to have a sense of technology. The founder was very adamant about her plans, but when I could not figure out what she was trying to do, I asked Anne to assist.

Anne continued to scratch her head and ask the same dogged questions over and over again. What is unique about what you are doing? Why is it worthy of protection? What will keep others out of the space? On and on this went until the client, in a fit of exasperation, declared that Anne simply didn't get it, implying that Anne's questioning was due to her failings and not something wrong with the business plan. After the client hung up, Anne told me her most basic client acceptance process—if she can't understand it, it is probably BS. It turned out that notwithstanding the client's extreme indignation that we could not understand her model—there never was any "there" there, and the company never did get off the ground.

It would have been a disaster for us to have taken that assignment. The best thing that could happen to the client would be to fail fast so she could move on to other more likely projects. Good people can explain what they are doing in five minutes, ten tops. If it sounds like BS, it probably is.

2.   What's in a Name?

DarrenCo (not its real name) came to me as a referral from a local angel investor who was actually acting as an advisor to the company. Like a lot of cutting-edge technology companies, this one's business model was hard to understand, and while the angel had been in business a long time, I knew that she had mostly lost money at it. I once joked that she had made a small fortune—out of her large fortune—but it was possible that many years of experience had given her new insights. She would provide the adult supervision to this company (i.e., the business acumen and experience needed to monetize a technology).

Based on her involvement, I took a meeting with Darren, the founder of DarrenCo.

The first meeting lasted two hours. The founder used so much industry jargon that it was hard to figure out what he had and what he was selling. One thing was clear—he had contacted everyone who was anyone that could act as a strategic partner for his mobile image projection technology. He had no contracts yet but lots of interest. Every time I asked about how he would make money with his patentable process, he would tell me about the big names (none of which I had heard of) that loved it and the big companies (which I had heard of) that were granting him meetings.

After the conclusion of the first meeting, I reread his materials and my notes and concluded that I needed another meeting with someone who was not so close to the technology to explain it and his model to me in plain English. I asked the angel to attend a second meeting while we drilled down on it. At that meeting, I again asked exactly how the company was going to make money with the technology.

Not surprisingly, the founder again started talking about all the companies that loved the idea of what they could do with his new whiz-bang thingamajig. It was clear that the founder was not the businessperson and his name-dropping was his way of saying that he did not know. What was surprising was the response from the angel, because she did the exact same thing. Instead of telling me that they could license the technology, manufacture devices, joint venture with other parties, sell ad space, or whatever, she echoed the thought that lots of people thought it was a cool idea.

In sum, they had no idea how they would make money with whatever they had. Can you guess how DarrenCo ended up?

As mentioned above, even a service provider has to triage potential clients, and a company that cannot articulate a monetization plan is not fundable. A company that cannot tell me how it will make money is DOA.

3.   Exit, Stage Left

David had the next big thing. His game concept was so unique and timely that it would blow away any game that had come before it. It was, he thought, a game changer (pun intended), and he went to work gathering his advisors, making plans, preparing projections, and so forth. In fact, it was such a great platform that he would build and build on it indefinitely. The idea of selling the company was not something that David thought much about since he was building a sustainable, socially useful product. David's enthusiasm for his product worked well with friends and family, who shared his vision and wanted to feel good about themselves by supporting a larger social purpose—and there was a huge market in games. There was enough potential upside to get a first meeting with a VC. We prepped well for the meeting, and everything went well until they asked the inevitable question about the company's exit plan.

Silence. There was a moment of dead air before the founder delivered his canned response about sale or IPO. That was enough to raise a red flag for the VC, and they drilled down on a major weakness in the plan. The fact was that, although we had formulated a plan, the founder did not believe it. He still held visions of not losing control of his baby for the indefinite future, even though a sale to a larger developer would make sense in this business. A founder who will not give up control or let the investors cash out equals DOA.

4.   I've Always Been Crazy but It's Kept Me From Going Insane

Craig was a technical genius. He had credentials, he was smart, and he was successful. Like a lot of brilliant people, however, Craig was a bit eccentric. In fact, it was his ability to see things unrestrained by conventional wisdom that made his new chip design so great.

My client was the angel fund that gave Craig his early stage funding. The manager of the angel group had known Craig for many years, so his eccentricities did not bother him. He knew they were harmless. For example, Craig was always unkempt and unshaven and even wore a rope instead of a belt. He was often seen barefoot. It was not that he could not afford a belt or shoes; it just never made sense to him to spend any money on such indulgences. Craig was a fierce Libertarian, and probably more of an anarchist if you pressed him on his political beliefs—but nobody ever did. He had also taken up a crusade against processed foods, would not eat sugar, and was a real pain to try to have lunch with because of the way he interrogated the waitress and cook about his meal. Despite these and all his other foibles, he was brilliant and did have a great chip design.

When the angel money came to a close, as expected, my client (Jack) had already had his golfing buddies in the clubby VC community lined up to take the company through the next round of funding. We cleaned Craig up for the meeting, and the PowerPoint presentation went well—although we were all holding our breath just a bit, hoping that the conversation would not drift toward politics, food, or the utility of belts and shoes. We were all quite relieved when we made it through the last slide with no weirdness. The VC was impressed. Craig answered all his questions brilliantly and succinctly. "Do you have an exit plan?" "Yes, we have an exit plan." "Would you step aside for an industry CEO?" "Of course I would step aside for your man as CEO."

We would probably get a term sheet. Then, as the meeting was coming to a close, the VC somewhat casually asked Craig what other interests he had—not as diligence but just to be personable. Craig started by saying, "Well, physics is my first love." We expected Craig to continue with a description of some arcane techie pursuit. "But my real interest is time travel," he continued.

Silence. The note gathering stopped. The VC sat back down in his chair. He stared for what seemed like a long time.

"What kind of travel?" he asked.

"Time travel." Craig beamed, happy that someone wanted to hear about his personal interests. "In fact," Craig continued, "you might want to invest in it. I hope to devote a lot more time and attention to time travel. You see, it works like this ..."

And then, there we were, riding the crazy train. The VC was half smiling politely, half not believing what he was hearing. Jack just sort of sank into his chair. I stopped billing. The company was now officially DOA.

Rule: Don't be crazy—or if you are crazy, try to keep that to yourself.

5. When the VCs Talk, Listen to Them

MobileSense (and that *is* its real name) made No Sense to me when I first heard about it. The founder, a brilliant software engineer named Yvonne, spent several hours patiently explaining the technology and business model that would allow mobile bookmarking of physical products. While I did not immediately "get" the business, I could see that Yvonne, a successful serial entrepreneur, knew what she was talking about, so I did what I vowed to never, ever do—work solely for equity.

After we formed a company around Yvonne's vision, we knocked on the door of every angel and VC in the Silicon Valley but soon discovered that the days of getting a Power Point funded were over—companies needed real traction in the Web 2.0 world. So, while we were not able to talk the institutions out of any cash dollars, we managed to get something even more valuable—their business advice. More accurately, we got their advice on what the company would have to look like to be fundable.

At each and every meeting, we came away with comments on what should be changed, what would work, and what would not work. We learned that going directly to publishing houses would be an expensive and probably ineffective go-to-market strategy. We learned where similar start-ups in the space had failed and why. We learned what sectors we needed to attack and what sectors were not worth the effort.

After a year of meetings and tweaking, MobileSense looked nothing like the original concept. Instead of targeting advertisers, we would target merchants. Instead of relying on subscription revenue, we would rely on click-through ad revenue. The VCs gave us no money, but they gave us a fundable business model. When we retooled and went back out for investment, we had a much better plan. As of this writing. MobileSense has raised angel money and is quickly gaining traction in its field.

6. Getting Funded

Assuming that you have not made any of the above mistakes and that you are indeed fundable, you will need to consider the options for raising money. MobileSense, described above, is a great example of the current process and evolution. Web 2.0 has dramatically changed the fundraising landscape. No longer does an idea require from $5 million to $10 million to prove itself. Almost any software or e-commerce idea can get launched with hundreds of thousands instead of millions of dollars. Software tools have become dirt cheap and readily accessible. The web has changed everything and may be the death knell for the VC industry (but *that's* a different book).

The typical company financing evolution is friends and family first, then angels and angel funds, followed by super angels and VCs, and then strategic investors. Of course, a great idea, solid company, and an experienced and credible team can "pass Go" and go directly to VCs or strategic investors, but the vast majority of companies will have to jump through the hoops.

a. Founders, Friends, and Fools

Companies need cash—there is no way around it, and the hope is that the company can get financeable before it breaks all the founders. Despite what you might have heard about using OPM (other people's money), the first source of funding will be the founders' own funds. I have seen a lot of founders mortgage their houses and "bet the farm" on their ideas, and as a lawyer, I discourage anyone from making any bets he or she cannot afford to lose, especially in this area. Keep in mind that no start-up company starts out to fail, but precious few succeed. Given the high risk/return ratio, a better strategy is to solicit small amounts from a larger pool of investors. Thus, rather than having a few founders dump their collective net worth into a venture, they might have a handful of friends and family members invest relatively small amounts, thus minimizing the pain if and when the venture fails. There is nothing at all wrong with this strategy, provided that a few simple rules (and about a million complex ones) are followed.

First, I wish I had a nickel for every nickel that was invested without adequate documentation. I know what you are thinking—you are taking money from friends. They trust you and would rather defer the legal expense of documentation than have you spend their money on legal fees. There are some problems with that approach. First, state corporate and securities laws require promoters to define and provide their investors with certificates or other evidences of ownership at the time of their investment and to make and obtain certain representations. A promoter who does not do so may be personally liable for the full amount of their investments.

Second, the failure to document investments raises "piercing the veil" issues and compromises the limited liability shield of the corporate form. Also, a lawyer may have difficulty giving a legal opinion as to securities law compliance when asked by the later institutional investors (as is commonly done) if those laws are ignored at the outset. This may not be a dead on arrival issue, but the cleanup might result in an escrow claim or a valuation hit, both of which are 100 percent avoidable.

The bigger, more realistic problem, however, is that memories change with twenty-twenty hindsight. Now, you might say with all sincerity that your boyfriend—who is "loaning" you your seed capital—would never, ever take advantage of you and claim that your verbal agreement is anything other than what you say it is, and I absolutely believe you. I know he would never do such a thing, not in a million years. But just to cover the statistically diminishingly small possibility that you might break up with him before you all become filthy rich, that he might act out of self-interest, or that you just might not have agreed to all the hairy details, we should paper the deal, just in case. You can blame it on your lawyer. And by the way, my experience is that undocumented seed money from a boyfriend or girlfriend leads to a dispute 100 percent of the time (but I know you will be the exception).

Issue number two has been touched on above, and that is the lack of securities law compliance. By now, you are probably familiar with the concept of an "accredited investor." In the case of an individual, that generally means a person who has a net worth of more than $1 million (excluding his or her principal residence) or annual income for the current and past two years of $200,000 ($300,000 jointly with spouse). That's interesting, but why do you care? Because in the United States, it is easier for a non-accredited investor to go to Las Vegas and bet his life savings away at a blackjack table than it is for him to spend it on stock in a privately held company.

If you sell securities to non-accredited investors in a sufficiently large enough amount, you must provide the investors with extensive information about the company, including its prospects, financials, risk factors, projections, and so forth. You do not have this problem with accredited-only investments (although you would want to provide all material information to comply with securities law antifraud rules). It is not the end of the world if you do have to provide a PPM (private placement memorandum) containing that information, it is just expensive and time-consuming—but it raises another less obvious problem.

When you close a VC financing at some point after the friends and family round, that financing will almost certainly be an accredited-only investment (no VC that I know of is not accredited). That fact allows the VC financing to go quickly and smoothly. If, however, the later accredited-only VC financing is integrated (or combined) with the earlier friends and family round, then the later round may be subject to the same disclosure requirements as a non-accredited round. That is an additional hassle that the parties will try to avoid.

It can get worse. When the company is ready to be sold, a potential buyer will have to deal with the non-accredited investors, so if the exit is a stock-for-stock acquisition, the acquirer will be issuing stock to non-accredited investors and will have the same issues as the company. Again, that is not the end of the world, but it raises compliance and transaction costs enough so that the alternative investment described above (i.e., gambling all your money away in Las Vegas) might not look like such a bad choice—it is certainly cheaper as a compliance matter. Don't blame me—write your congressman.

To be more specific, Rule 504 of "Regulation D"[27] provides an exemption for the offer and sale of up to $1 million of securities in a twelve-month period. Rule 505 provides an exemption for offers and sales of securities totaling up to $5 million in any twelve-month period to an unlimited number of "accredited investors" and up to thirty-five "unaccredited investors." Rule 506 allows an unregistered sale of securities to an unlimited number of accredited investors and up to thirty-five other purchasers; however, all non-accredited investors must be "sophisticated" (must have sufficient knowledge and experience in financial and business matters to make them capable of evaluating the merits and risks of the prospective investment).

As a practical matter, the benefit of Rules 504–506 is actually found in Rule 502(b)(1), which provides that the company need not provide the extensive information normally required when sales are made under Rules 504–506, or to accredited investors. Many start-up companies seek to avoid the costs of

---

[27] 17 C.F.R. §230.501 et seq.

compliance and will exclude non-accredited investors in pursuit of that goal, as well as avoiding the problems described above.

However, many start-up companies will rely on their non-accredited friends and family to help them fund the company. Are those companies DOA if they do so? Probably not, but if they exceed the above limitations, they must incur the additional expense of meeting the information requirements through the preparation of a detailed private placement memorandum, and they may have to deal with the possibility of a later institutional round being aggregated with the earlier round—thus vitiating the earlier round.

Since so much rides on the definition of "accredited investor," it is worth mentioning the requirements here. Generally, for an individual to qualify as an accredited investor, he or she must either earn an individual income of more than $200,000 per year, or a joint (with their spouse) income of $300,000, in each of the last two years and expect to reasonably maintain the same level of income; have a net worth exceeding $1 million, either individually or jointly with his or her spouse; or be a general partner, executive officer, or director of the issuer. Recent changes in the law *exclude* the value of a principal residence in the net worth determination, so it is more difficult now than earlier to meet this definition.

So, how do you know if investors are "accredited"? Basically, you ask them by requiring them to fill out an investor suitability questionnaire (ISQ). That questionnaire will also tease out whether or not they meet sophistication standards in case they are not accredited. Two pieces of practical wisdom are appropriate here. I have found over the years that people will lie on an ISQ, and others will buy securities on behalf of their non-accredited friends. As a founder, you should not tolerate either approach.

First, an issuer may *reasonably* rely on the ISQ, so if someone is obviously lying, the company should not accept his or her conclusions without further diligence. Second, the purchaser may be required to represent that he or she is acquiring the securities on his or her own behalf. If in fact the purchaser is not, the purchase could create problems for the company under rules prohibiting the syndication of securities or the limitations on the number of stockholders that a nonreporting company is allowed to have.[28] Honesty may not always be the best policy, but it is the least risky in this area. Stay within these rules and turn down money if you have to.

b.   Venture Capital

The Holy Grail of the start-up company world is venture capital. There is a belief that getting funded by an institution that dares to call itself a venture capital firm will be validation enough to almost guarantee success. After all, these guys did not get rich by betting on losers. They will take their share, and when the time is right, they will call their golfing buddies in the investment banking business—and the next thing you know, the company will exit in an IPO or acquisition, and everyone will be awash in cash.

The reality, of course, is much different, and a good rule of thumb to follow is to never, ever take VC money except as a last resort. Yes, it is true that they may have access to cash for follow-on rounds, and they may have connections that lead to liquidity, and they may even be able to add value beyond the dollars invested, *but* you, the founder, may not see much of all that great value by the time the company exits.

First, although you will not usually give up control in the first round (Series A), not many companies get to liquidity after only one round. If your company is that good, that is all the more reason to find friendlier cash. Otherwise, plan on doing a Series B round, and plan on losing control at that point. If you are still the founding CEO by then, plan on finding a new job after the founders have lost control. It is a rare CEO that stays with the company from formation to exit after multiple rounds,

---

[28] Securities Exchange Act of 1934 Rule 12g5-1.

and VCs are not known for keeping officers around for senti-mental reasons. To be fair, the skill set that a CEO needs to launch a company is probably not the skill set needed to manage that same company once it reaches the middle market. Just hope that you are fully or mostly vested by the time you get the hook.

Second, even if you do not lose control, the VCs (and any other Series A preferred stock investors) will have a liquidation preference in their stock. That means that when the company is sold, they get paid first. If the company does multiple rounds, there will be multiple preferences, so not only do the founders' percentages get diluted as the company matures, but the amount that the company must be sold for before the founders see any money increases. More than one founder has ended up working for the VCs with no real hope of covering the preferences. There is a way around that result, which is described later in this chapter.

Next, do not expect VCs to want to exit at the same time as you do. If you have given them redemption rights (commonly requested) or a drag along,[29] the VCs will have the (theoretical) ability to force a sale of the company. Keep in mind that they have many other investments that demand their time, so their tolerance for distraction may not be the same as that of the founders. In other words, the investors will often cut their losses and force a sale of the company before the founders are ready.

Expect to have a board that you are now accountable to. That board may or may not agree with your ("your" being "the founders'") views on how to run the business, but the members will not be shy in offering their opinions and demanding answers if things do not go right. Depending on what managerial rights

---

[29] A drag along is a right to force a stockholder to sell shares. For example, if an investor desires to sell its shares to a third party, but the third party wants all but not less than all of the shares of stock in the company, if the investor has a drag along right with respect to the shares that it does not own, it would have a right to force the other shareholders to participate in the sale to the third party.

they negotiate, the founders may find the VCs quite involved in their day-to-day business.

All of the above issues are manageable, but there is one issue that is not. Probably the worst thing about VC money is that it comes with extremely high expectations. The economics of VC funds require huge returns on rather large investments. If it turns out that your company is not going to generate those huge returns, the investor may want to exit early and deploy elsewhere. Those skewed economics can make for unfortunate company dynamics if things do not work out according to plan.

c. Finders

There is no discussion I hate more than the one we must have about professional finders. First, a word about terms. A "finder" is a person who finds investors for a company. He does not negotiate terms. He does not effect transactions in securities. He just finds. In theory, at least, a finder is exempt from registration as a broker. This is a narrow exemption, as the following factors are characteristic of brokers, not finders: participating in negotiations, counseling investors on the merits of investing, recommending the investment to investors, receiving percentage compensation, holding securities or cash, providing details of the financing to investors, and conducting sales efforts.

Even if the finder does not engage in the foregoing activities, he still may be engaged in effecting transactions in securities and therefore fall outside the "finder's exemption" if he receives transaction-based compensation more than once or twice in his career. Nevertheless, most lawyers are content to hold their noses and go along with the company's assertion that their finders are truly "finders." Or, at least, they were until the SEC recently came down hard on some purported finders.

Some states, such as California, have their own finder's exemption to broker dealer registration. Under federal as well as California law, paying success-based compensation is a factor that contraindicates finder status. The fact that percentage compensation is used is an important (and maybe determinative) factor, and the safest course of action (other than using only registered brokers) is to pay fixed fees and not percentage or contingent compensation. If that is not practical, what are the risks?

First, the investor would have a claim against the unlicensed broker for violation of the registration requirement. The company may also be liable as an aider and abettor of the violation of the broker registration requirements, which may be a showstopper for any company that plans to issue securities in a public offering. The investor would also have a right to get its money back, and the use of an unregistered broker could result in a failure of the company to comply with securities law exemptions from registration.

The use of unregistered brokers has ugly legal consequences all around, and the worst part is that it might not do much good. Many institutional investors hate the idea of dealing with finders on the theory that any company worth its charter should not need to try that hard to raise money. Of course, this perception will depend on the identity of the finder and the strength of his or her relationships with the investment community. This is a real issue given that pretty much anyone can claim to be a finder. If you choose to go this route, choose carefully, and be cautious.

Finally, the finder's agreement itself should be vetted by legal counsel, but often it is not (by definition, the company does not have money to hire lawyers). These agreements are usually poorly drafted and outrageously one sided. For example, think long and hard before granting anything that looks like exclusive rights (especially without a corresponding process guideline) to anyone, or you may find yourself paying twice for the same money, or paying someone who did nothing. You would be surprised how often this happens. In fact, an entire industry expects it to happen.

There is a school of thought that the use of a finder who takes a percentage of funds raised for finding VC money must fail by definition since a VC does not want 6 percent of the investment going right out the door to someone whose only value is having a deep rolodex. In response, a new kind of finder has emerged in recent years—one that takes cash at hourly rates and equity for his or her services and adds significant value in the form of counsel and advice. That advice will include helping with the business plan, PowerPoint deck, and executive summary, as well as coaching the founders on their pitch. That kind of help can be invaluable since, while a good pitch might not get you funded, a bad pitch will kill it. Many times, I have sat through a PowerPoint presentation that lost the VCs by the fourth slide. Note that if they start checking their smartphones during the pitch, it is all over.

The new finders do not take a percentage of the funds raised and, therefore, do not give investors the impression that they are talking to a company that is so hard up for money that it had to hire a finder to find money for them. They also may invest their own money, making them at least cherubs if not angels. These are valuable people to have on board (but not necessarily on "the board") if the company can afford to pay a small amount since the additional assistance frees management to focus on the business and avoids wasting hard-to-get face time with investors in their "one-shot-at-it" meetings. From a legal standpoint, using this type of finder also avoids those pesky broker problems since they are paid hourly (percentage compensation is the single worst factor). Hire them if you can.

d.   Angels

An "angel" is a professional investor who offers financial support to a seed or start-up company after the company has exhausted the support of friends and family but before the company requires a larger institutional investment. Angels are most often accredited individuals with entrepreneurial backgrounds but may also be funds or groups of individuals. Angels also theoretically offer advice to their companies and may have experience starting or operating companies.

In terms of attractiveness, angel money is second only to funding through operations. Angels tend to go easier on the company on terms than VC and financial investors and do not invest enough to justify the mind-numbing due diligence that bureaucratic, pencil-pushing strategic investors will put you through. They also tend to be more aligned with management than later stage investors because they get in early at low valuations.

In recent years, the angels have become more and more organized in order to leverage their group knowledge and contacts. Companies are now routinely asked to present to "angel groups." The benefit of such groups is that angels are more readily accessible to entrepreneurs, and the combined knowledge of numerous angels in a group more effectively screens entrepreneurs for appropriate investment opportunities. Angel groups often target particular industries, geographical areas, or specific purposes. Angel groups can assume different legal structures, including but not limited to the following: (1) nonprofit corporations, (2) 501(c) tax-exempt corporations, (3) C corporations, (4) subchapter S corporations, (5) limited liability companies, (6) limited partnerships, (7) limited liability partnerships, and (8) informal arrangements.

Angel groups look for a steady flow of investment opportunities, or "deal flow." The groups conduct an initial screening of companies, considering such factors as the nature of the company, corporate structure, management team, contractual relationships, financial profile and operation, ownership of intellectual property, and third-party validation. Angel groups then invite the entrepreneurs to pitch their companies at their regular group meetings.

Almost every angel group has an online presentation process and may insist that a company apply through that process. Resist that process if you can since it is not the best way to approach an angel or any other group. A typical angel group will get hundreds or thousands of plans and summaries a year, and it simply will not give them all the attention they deserve. The investment business, even at the angel level, is a personal business, and the best way to get in front of an angel is to be introduced by someone who knows the angel personally, such as your lawyer or advisor. I know of numerous cases in which a company submitted a business plan that was rejected or (more often) simply ignored but the company was then granted a meeting after being introduced by the right person.

After an entrepreneur has presented to the group of potential investors, the group or individual investors (depending on the group structure) will engage in a financial valuation of the company, which may be accomplished by reference to book value, market value, income value, or expected return on investment ("first-stage diligence"). After financial valuation, an analysis of legal documents, facilities, management structure, and employees will be conducted, referred to as the "due diligence" process ("second-stage diligence"). At second-stage diligence, the investor will dive deeper, and the company may disclose the "secret sauce" of its technology, trade secrets, and business and market data.

If the company survives these two latter phases of scrutiny, angels will consider making an investment. Typically, the first stage precedes a term sheet, and the second stage commences with the execution of a term sheet. You should not get anywhere near second-stage diligence without a nondisclosure agreement (NDA).

A Word About "Fishing." My father used to say that "nice guys finish last," and nowhere is this more evident than in the institutional investment community. Any experienced founder will have stories to share about this. One of the more pernicious practices to be wary of is the general "fishing" for information in which industry-targeted groups will engage under the guise of evaluating an investment. Sometimes, the investor has already placed its bets in the space and just wants to know what the competition is doing, where the industry is going, or what new ideas he or she can steal.

Knowing who is for real and who is fishing can be difficult, but there are a few red flags. If the investor has already invested in a competitor, he or she may be fishing. If the investor has a lot of questions about business models, markets, and technology but not about valuation, rights, and preferences, he or she may be fishing. If the investor knows more about your business than you do, he or she may not need you and may just be fishing. Other than looking for these markers, there is no real way of knowing, and while some states (like California) impose an affirmative obligation of good faith and fair dealing, are you really going to try to sue the rich investor who may or may not have gotten an idea from you? The best you can do is to get a good NDA (if he or she will sign it) and avoid those investors who experience or intuition tells you are disingenuous.

After an angel investor has decided to invest, the parties must determine the terms, usually documented in a term sheet. Angel investors typically contribute between $25,000 and $100,000 in each company of their choice, and groups expect individual angels to contribute a certain amount annually to their choice of presenting entrepreneurs.

The two standard forms of investment are debt and equity. A debt investment may be secured or unsecured, and convertible or not convertible. An equity investment means common or preferred stock. Sometimes the term "private equity investment" is used to describe a contribution of funds to a nonpublic company in exchange for an equity or debt security, such as preferred stock or notes.

Investment may occur on an individual or a group level. Investment on a group level often involves "pooled" funds. An investor that refers to itself as a "fund" indicates an entity in which multiple investors have contributed capital for the purpose of investment.

After making an investment, an angel investor may demand an active role within the company, such as a position on the board of directors, or he or she may simply request information rights, such as the regular receipt of company reports and financial statements. Entrepreneurs should communicate with their angel investors regularly and in a timely manner, relaying quarterly updates, company progress, and issues.

A Word About Information. For whatever reason, companies tend to be more secretive about their financial information, and investors tend to be more paranoid, than either of them should be. Millions of dollars in legal fees could be saved if companies would disclose and investors would not draw conspiracy theories out of a company's failure to disclose.

The typical scenario is as follows. Start-up Inc. is overwhelmed with work. The founders must get the beta product out or website up, they must get to market, and they must spend time searching for the next round of funding. Spending a lot of time preparing financial reports is not their biggest priority, and management may not have spare time to talk to the angel investors about all of their bright ideas on how to run things. After all, the investors trusted them enough to make the initial investment; they certainly should trust them to spend it without constant oversight.

From the investors' point of view, however, it seems like Start-up Inc. was all over them when they needed money, and once they got it, the investors cannot seem to get a call returned. The investors think, "Where are the financials that we were promised? What do you suppose they are doing with all that money, and why don't they want me to know?"

It gets worse when the investors can get together and ruminate about the "lack of transparency." Soon enough, Start-up Inc. will get a letter from someone like me that "demands" a long list of information and sets arbitrary deadlines. When a company gets a letter like that, the smart thing to do is to *give them the information.* The law requires it, business practice compels it, and as distracting as it is, it is far less distracting than what can happen when a company stonewalls its investors for information (i.e., litigation).

The smart start-ups give up the information. The rest of them either ignore the demand letter (bad idea) or get competitive.

"Who does this investor think he is to go around 'demanding' me to do stuff?" the entrepreneur might think. "I've got real work to do. They don't appreciate how hard I am working to make them money. Screw those guys. Maybe I will just quit if that's the way they are going to be."

The law requires that corporations hold annual meetings and provide certain information to shareholders. Section 211(b) of the Delaware General Corporation Law, for example, generally requires annual meetings (or a consent in lieu thereof). Many start-up companies are not very diligent about complying with that particular formality since the disgruntled stockholder's remedy for noncompliance is to go to court and obtain an order requiring an annual meeting. In twenty-eight years of practice, I have never seen anyone do that.

The law also requires that corporations provide certain information to shareholders. Section 220 of the Delaware General Corporation Law, for example, allows any shareholder the right to "inspect" books and records. As a practical matter, companies will (and should) simply provide the information to the demanding shareholders rather than insisting that they wheel in their own photocopy machine. The requested information must be for a "proper purpose" (a low standard), and the demand must meet certain formalities. Very little imagination is required to find a "proper purpose" for a shareholder request. Often a company will be most concerned that the purpose is not the disclosure of their information to a competitor, and the company will condition the delivery of that information on the execution by the requesting stockholder of an NDA.

e.   Incubators and "Mentor" Capital

Recently, various forms of incubators have emerged as a significant force in the start-up company world. Many incubators will provide space and administrative support to a promising idea to help get it off the ground. Many organizations will provide a small amount of seed capital. All will offer opportunities for connecting with investors, advisors, other entrepreneurs, and service providers. Many are focused on companies from outside the United States and are supported by their home country governments. Some organizations do not go so far as to provide facilities but go beyond providing just capital; they also provide mentorship, or, "mentor capital."

In all of these cases, the company is receiving not only money but also expertise, connections, and links. The relatively large amounts of equity that are given to these organizations reflect the value of the intangibles that accompany the hard cash.

f.   RoyseLink

Several resource sites now allow founders to interact with angels and investors in an online searchable environment. AngelList and Gust are two such sites. Some of the resource sites have a qualification process to get on the site; others are more like a directory.

My firm has created its own version of an exclusive site that will match selected client companies with our contacts in the angel and VC community, as well as access to Royse Law Firm's network of service providers and advisors. RoyseLink is found at www.RoyseLink.com. The benefit of sites such as RoyseLink is that they are exclusive—I screen all listed companies and select those on the site. In effect, if the company is on the site, it has already passed one level of review. Thereafter, a company that is accepted to the site can request an introduction to a particular VC or angel and, if I think it is an appropriate match, I will make that introduction. On the investor side, the founders' summaries are searchable, so a VC can periodically review the companies listed on the RoyseLink site for matches. RoyseLink takes what I have been doing in a real-world environment for the past 20 years and places it into an online virtual environment.

g. Strategic Investors

Strategic investors differ in a few respects from angels and VCs. First, by "strategic" investor, we mean an operating company as opposed to a passive investment fund or family office, and the person is investing not just for the potential financial return but also due to some reason that relates to the investor's core business. That reason might be to secure a source of supply of materials or products, to strengthen a relationship with a customer, or to acquire an "in" in an aspect of an industry.

In fact, the main "strategic" goal may be acquisition, but the investor may not be ready to acquire 100 percent of the company. That may be because the target company does not believe that its valuation is all that it can be, or it may be that the investor is not convinced that the target company is the best bet it can make in that particular market segment. Whatever the reason, the strategic investor almost always requests a right of first offer, right of first refusal, or right of notification with respect to a sale of the company's business.

Keep in mind that the strategic investor wants the company, not a minority position in a privately held company, so it will try to find ways to acquire that business. Thus, expect one of those three rights in the strategic investor's term sheet, followed by indignation, hand-wringing, and name-calling by the company's VC investors (if there are any) who, no matter how many times it happens to them, will insist that it is off-the-charts unreasonable.

A Few Words about Terminology. A right of first refusal means that the company must first offer its assets or securities to the investor before it can offer those securities or assets to anyone else. In effect, this chills or kills any possibility of there being a third-party offer, since who wants to do the diligence to make an offer if someone else is going to take the opportunity?

A similar right is a "preemptive right," although technically, that is a bit different from a right of first refusal. A preemptive right is the right of current shareholders to maintain their percentage ownership of a company by buying a proportionate number of shares of any future issue of stock. Instead of a traditional, antiquated preemptive right, most term sheets will grant the investors a right to maintain their percentage interest, and, in fact, some issuances will require investors to purchase their pro rata shares of later issuances or suffer severe dilution (see below). This is not the buzzkill that a right of first refusal is since there is still room for third party-investment, even with a right to maintain.

A first right of negotiation is the proper counter when a strategic investor proposes a right of first refusal. A first right of negotiation simply provides that if the company gets a third-party offer to buy stock or assets, it will notify the investor and allow it to negotiate in good faith to bid. There is no obligation for the company to take the strategic investor's offer (unlike a right of first refusal), but it probably would do so if it matched the third party's offer. Thus, it is not a great solution—but it is a better one than the right of first refusal.

A right of notification simply gives the strategic investor a right to be notified of any financing or acquisition proposals. The strategic investor then, theoretically, will know when a company is "in play" and can insert itself into the process. A point to watch is that the right of notification should not conflict with any confidentiality agreement that the company may be asked to sign with a third-party investor. The company may find itself bound by two contracts that, logically, cannot both be complied with.

One thing to avoid in all of these scenarios is a lock-up or no-shop clause that holds up the company during the negotiation or notification period. The compromise is usually a limitation on the time and scope of the strategic investor's rights. For example, the company might agree to give the strategic investor notice of any third-party offers and might also agree to negotiate with it—but only for a short period of time and only with respect to certain types of offers (e.g., a sale of assets to a competitor). There is no easy answer to this one, and a right of notification may be the best you can do. The strength of this provision translates directly to exit value since it will affect the ability to sell the company for the highest dollar on the back end. The company should remain mindful of that fact.

How Much Diligence Is Due? One of the most surprising experiences for a founder is the due diligence process. First-time founders are invariably surprised at the lengths to which institutional investors will go to learn all about them. Gone is the "of-course-I-trust-you" optimism of the early meetings, and instead, the entrepreneurs will find themselves being subjected to the legal equivalent of a proctology exam. And it does not end at the diligence stage—it continues and extends to the representations and warranties that the founders will be required to make to the investor in the securities purchase agreements.

Thus, the question always comes up about what is necessary to disclose. The answer is ... *everything*.

Or, to be more precise, everything that is *material* to the investor, which begs the question of what is considered material.

One helpful rule of thumb that many lawyers use is that if you would rather the investor not know something, it is probably material. My own rule is that if you have to ask, it is probably material. In other words, when in doubt, disclose. Is that five-year-old DUI material? I don't know, so let's disclose. You got a letter from a lawyer claiming trademark infringement? That is definitely material. Girlfriend on the payroll? That might be material, so let's disclose. You like to wear women's underwear? That is probably *not* material, and I don't even need to know that.

You get the idea.

Chapter 7

Contractors, Consultants, and Strategic Partners

At its fundamental core, most start-ups create value by taking existing technologies and combining them in ways that are new or more marketable. Thus, almost from the start, the start-up company will engage with third parties for access to technology, expertise, or markets. Much of the value of a company will be attributable to the strength of its contractual relationships, and that is partly a legal concern. In fact, the agreements described in this chapter so directly impact value that only the most feckless company would execute any such agreement without legal counsel.

Not only are a company's contracts a large part of its value, they may also be a large part of what detracts from its value if not properly drafted. A contract may give away valuable IP, for example, or may impose unreasonable risk on a company. Thus, contract negotiation and drafting is as much a defensive exercise as a value-building one. Here are a few important provisions to pay attention to.

a. Confidentiality and Nondisclosure

A confidentiality clause may be included in another more comprehensive agreement or be set forth on a stand-alone basis as an NDA (nondisclosure agreement or confidentiality agreement). In either case, the concepts are similar, and the discussion of NDAs includes confidentiality clauses in other agreements.

NDA. An NDA is one of the most important three-letter acronyms that a start-up entrepreneur can know. Under an NDA, one or more parties will agree not to disclose confidential and/or proprietary information to third parties. It is essential for a few reasons that may not be completely obvious.

First of all, and most significantly, an NDA is a sort of non-compete agreement in that the receiving party will (or should) agree not to use the covered information for any purposes other than as contemplated by other agreements. For example, if the parties are contemplating a partnering or alliance agreement, the NDA may state that the covered information may only be used to evaluate that relationship, so that if the deal falls through, the receiving party will not take that information and use it to compete with the disclosing party. Enforcement and proof may be another matter, but at least the parties will have contractually bound themselves not to use the covered information for any reason other than as contemplated.

Second, many companies' technology is protected by state trade secret law rather than patents. In other words, the thing that prevents any Tom, Dick, or Harry from taking a company's technology and starting his own company is the fact that it is secret, and Tom, Dick, or Harry could be legally prevented from using that information. For example, a business plan may not be patentable, but it may be essential to the start-up company's success. Consider all the great ideas that could have easily been implemented by someone else if he or she had just figured out the business model. How could those companies have hired contractors, solicited funding, or established a business presence without someone somewhere stealing their trade secrets?

Under the law of trade secrets, a secret is a secret only if the owner has taken reasonable steps to protect it from disclosure. "Duh!" you might say, but this simplistic concept has tremendous legal significance. Large corporations take this rule very seriously and restrict access to IP by extensive means, which are chronicled in written manuals and procedures—and will invariably include a requirement that anyone with access to confidential information execute an NDA.

Granted, a secret may be secret even without an NDA. A party may be legally prohibited from using someone's idea based on unfair trade practice laws even without an NDA, but that type of claim to ownership is not fundable. That is why a failure to protect trade secrets with NDAs might be a DOA issue.

Now that we have seen why a good NDA, or a confidentiality clause in a consulting agreement, is important, let's discuss what should go into it.

Scope. The NDA should clearly define what is protected. Broad, general language is a good start (such as the phrase "all confidential or proprietary information"), but it helps to specify what specific documents or language will be included, such as business plans, technical information, employee data, marketing data, and so forth, in whatever form. The discloser would like to protect all disclosures, including oral disclosures, while a recipient may attempt to limit it to documents clearly marked as confidential. If the latter course is chosen, the discloser must remember to mark its confidential documents.

Exclusions. Almost all standard forms carve out from the NDA some version of the following information:

1. Information that is in the public domain

2. Information that is known to the recipient at the time of disclosure

3. Information that is disclosed with the prior written approval of the discloser

4. Information from a source other than the discloser

5. Information that is disclosed pursuant to the order of a court, administrative agency, or other governmental body

Various aspects of the above exclusions are sometimes negotiated, such as notice and evidentiary or proof matters, but an important point is to not stress out over these exclusions, as they are—for the most part—standard.

If your company is the recipient of the information, however, one exception that should be noted is a right to disclose information to your advisors. It may be implied, but you want the right to disclose information to your lawyer or accountant for evaluation purposes. The best practice is to spell that out rather than risk a claim of a violation.

Representatives. It does not do much good to have an NDA with a company if it can get around it by using an affiliate. Granted, there may be some breach of a covenant of good faith and fair dealing, or there may be some other legal basis for preventing a company from disclosing confidential information to another party who uses it in violation of the NDA, but that is hardly satisfactory as a drafting matter. The NDA must obligate the recipient of the confidential information to require any persons to whom he or she discloses confidential information to be similarly obligated to keep the information confidential. Companies have and will establish empty shell companies to execute NDAs to limit their exposure for breach, which is not a recipe for building trust with a future partner.

Nonsolicit Agreements. I like to include nonsolicit clauses in the NDA. This clause will prevent the recipient from raiding employees, customers, or even vendors. Arguably, the scope restriction on what the recipient can do with the information might cover this issue, but again, I like to spell out that the recipient cannot use confidential information such as employee salary data to solicit employees or confidential customer data to solicit the company's customers.

In some states, such as California, an agreement not to compete may be difficult to enforce other than in connection with the sale of the goodwill of a business. However, there is a fine and important distinction between using confidential information to compete and actually competing. While a bare agreement not to compete might not be enforceable, the disclosing party can prevent the recipient from competing by prohibiting the use of the discloser's confidential information to solicit customers. The nonsolicit clause should always be phrased that way.

Similarly, a nonsolicit agreement is risky in states that protect the rights of employees to work. An agreement not to solicit might not be enforceable. Worse, it might give rise to a claim of unfair trade practices by the employee against both contracting companies (welcome to California!). However, an agreement not to use confidential information to solicit would not cover responses to general solicitations (like a newspaper ad).

Term. An NDA will usually specify the "term" of the agreement. In other words, the NDA will state that the recipient will be subject to nondisclosure obligations for a period of X years, X being a negotiated time period. For many companies, X years is a lifetime, and anything disclosed now will be worthless in X years. For those companies, a "term" clause is as far as they need go. For companies that are disclosing trade secrets that have a longer shelf life than X years, however, a term clause may be interpreted to surrender trade secret rights that they otherwise might have had. Absent an agreement, the right to prohibit the use of their trade secret information under relevant trade secret law would last for as long as the information is secret (and not otherwise end at the expiration of X years). Thus, those companies should clarify that the NDA is not intended to replace any rights that the company has under applicable trade secret law. This is a subtle but important legal point.

A Word About Assignment. If your company is the recipient and not the discloser, its NDA, even more than other agreements, should be assignable to acquirers. A typical company will enter into numerous NDAs during its life prior to an exit by acquisition, and having to obtain consents to assignment of all of its NDAs can be a real hassle.

As you can see, this is a subtle area. Missing one of these points may not make you DOA, but a bad noncompete could be a valuation issue.

b.　IP Ownership

Few items are as heavily debated in a contractor agreement as ownership of technology rights. The addition of the "ownership" language is more important in the consulting or alliance context where technology is being developed than in the context of an agreement (such as with a financier) where information is merely being disclosed in order for the recipient to evaluate some other arrangement (such as a financing). In that former scenario, the service recipient or licensee will usually want ownership of whatever is being created while the alliance partner will seek to carve out tools and proprietary items that he or she previously owned or is developing for repeated use, such as templates, designs, or forms. Much of the negotiation in this area relates to what can be used again and again by the developer.

Even though the law would otherwise grant the contractor ownership rights in the results of his or her services, that result can be changed by contract. Counterintuitively, just because you hired someone to develop something for you—like a website— does not mean that you own it. If the developer is an employee, the employer may own the developed product as a "work for hire." If that service provider is not an employee—but is instead a partner or contractor—the person paying for the work may only have a nonexclusive license to use what the contractor has developed.

This means that he can then take the result of the work you paid for and sell it to the next guy, who may be your competitor. Not only does this detract from the value of your company, but it is done every day. For example, many contracts I draft start with the last form I worked on and use some text or wording or knowledge that I picked up working on a similar contract for someone else. It is a rare client who is savvy enough to insist on ownership of the work product itself (he or she usually just wants a certain result), and it would be rarer still for a lawyer to agree to that grant. This is why contracts take on a standard form, especially within a law firm. Many of the contracts described in this chapter are such standard forms.

An example of this came home to me a few years ago when I agreed to draft some template contracts for a software developer. Because of his background in IP, he reasonably asked me to agree that he would own all rights to the work product, including the templates. In other words, he did not want me to take a form that I created on his nickel and sell it again as is universally done by lawyers. The documents that we were creating were unique enough that I did not feel imposed upon by agreeing to do it his way, but it turned a large project into a huge one since I was forced to grow every word from scratch in the documents. That is the world in which most businesses operate, and the parties must take care that they understand what rights they are giving away when they enter into these agreements. This factor definitely affects the value of its agreements and the value of the company.

c.   Indemnification

Suppose that you, the developer company, agree to indemnify the contracting company for any damages arising out of claims for infringement of any intellectual property that you transfer to them. You know what you are developing and have no reason to believe that any of it infringes on someone else's IP rights. Is it reasonable to give that indemnity in those circumstances?

To answer that question, you have to imagine the worst case scenario. If the deliverable is patentable but not patented, a third-party patent could issue and result in the contractor not being able to use the delivered technology—or at least having to pay for a license. The fact that the technology might have been independently developed will be of no help to the defendant in that patent infringement lawsuit. If the owner of the patent does not agree to a license, the contractor may not be able to use the technology at all. What is that problem worth to a lawyer suing for damages? The answer is an amount that is limited only by a jury's imagination. In other words, the developer's one dollar of revenue might cost $1 million in lost profits. Before you dismiss this as a remote business risk, keep in mind that this happens all the time. I have seen a company confronted with a billion dollar lost profits claim in this very scenario.

Depending on whom you represent, this is classic business risk allocation. The way that the developer would protect himself is to limit any claims to a "knowing" infringement, so if a patent that was unknown by the developer at the time of contract pops up at some point down the road, the developer does not get stuck with that cost. Another solution is to cap damages. The maximum damages that a developer can be required to pay are often limited by some metric tied to consideration payable under the contract. Without knowledge qualifiers and damage caps, this issue definitely could be a company killer for a developer.

Chapter 8

International Operations

These days, not even a Ford car is wholly made in the United States. Companies go international from the get-go. Lately, more and more investment capital is from foreign sources as well, raising additional tax and legal structuring possibilities.

International expansion comes in various flavors. Almost every company will consider outsourcing certain functions to foreign contractors or affiliates to achieve cost or other efficiencies. In addition, some companies will look offshore for new markets. Of course, the outbound company must consider the effects of foreign law, and should have competent foreign counsel on board. With foreign operations, often the tricky part is knowing what questions to ask, as illustrated in the following story.

a.   Foreign Legal Issues

I had been on the phone for at least two hours now with a Swedish lawyer. Our mutual US client was trying to reorganize their Scandinavian operations and we were seeking a tax-free way to do so. The tax issue was a foreign one and, as US counsel, we were relying on our foreign counsel to provide guidance. He shot down every idea that I came up with. How about a stock-for-stock exchange? "No, that is taxable under Swedish law." How about a merger? "Taxable." An asset transfer? "Taxable." And so it went until I had exhausted all my bright ideas. Then just as I was about to give up, I asked "Is there any way to conclude this transaction on a tax-free basis?"

"Yes," came the reply. "The foreign affiliate can sell its interest for a dollar."

Although it would have been nice if he had told me that at the start, the lesson is that foreign law is not US law, and things we may take for granted in the US do not necessarily hold true in other countries. Tax is a big issue, but there are numerous other issues. Any company seeking to expand to foreign countries should be cognizant of these issues:

1. Tax. Most of the world will tax a US company on the earnings of its office in country. The US has income tax treaties that require the US company to have a permanent establishment in the target country before it may be taxable there, but treaty benefits typically must be claimed. In addition, countries vary on what they view as a permanent establishment. Some countries (such as South Korea and India) take a surprisingly broad view of this phrase. Even if the US company does not have a PE, it may still be subject to withholding taxes on payments from the target country, such as royalties, dividends, interest and payments for services.

2. VAT—value added tax. Many industrialized countries impose a value added tax on goods and services. A VAT is a tax on the incremental value in a product at each stage of production or sale. There are several different kinds of VAT and portions may or may not be refundable; thus, foreign tax planning often includes a component of VAT planning.

3. Employment. Many US companies have received a hard lesson in the employment laws of foreign jurisdictions. In some countries, it is exceedingly difficult

to fire an employee without paying excessive amounts of severance. Some counties mandate high levels of benefits and retirement contributions. For these and other reasons, US companies are often advised to enter a foreign country through a wholly owned subsidiary instead of directly as a branch office.

4. Contractual Provisions. One of the fundamental tenets of US contract law is "freedom of contract," meaning that parties should be free to strike whatever deal they want and the courts should enforce that deal. That is not necessarily the case in foreign countries. For example, I have had clients find out the hard way that many European countries will supply their own rules regarding damages on termination of a distributor contract. Before you cleverly decide to avoid those rules by agreeing that US law will apply, you should know that those countries may also legislate which law applies, regardless of what a party thought they agreed to. Contracting within a foreign country can be a tar baby for the unadvised.

5. IP Protection. This is the big one for many companies. The lack of enforcement of anti-piracy laws in China and other countries is well known and, while enforcement has been stepped up in the biggest offenders, a US company may decide (and many often do) to avoid public registrations (such as patent filings), or to keep the knowledge base (meaning the people and processes) in a country that will provide legal protection.

6. Privacy. The US and other countries have privacy standards, meaning that there are rules around the protections that companies must take to ensure the confidentiality of personal information (such as employee data). Privacy standards in the US are not as stringent as the standards required in other countries.

Thus, some US companies have found that they are legally prohibited from managing foreign information from the US affiliate. In fact, privacy is a factor to consider when deciding where to locate a foreign base company.

7. Currency Controls. Many countries (notably China) have restrictions on the movement of funds out of the country.

8. Liability Issues. Some mobile businesses (such as internet companies) tend to be organized in foreign jurisdictions to limit their exposure to US claims. High-risk businesses such as companies that deal in adult content, for example, might seek to limit their connection to US states, and exposure to US courts, by incorporating their operating company in a remote jurisdiction and moving business operations outside the US.

As should be obvious from this short summary, entering a foreign market or establishing a foreign source may implicate numerous rules that may have surprising and adverse consequences. Foreign counsel should be consulted on all relevant foreign legal issues.

b.   Foreign structures

If a company does have the metrics to establish offshore operations, it is better off doing that sooner rather than later for reasons discussed below. An international company must consider the costs of incorporation, the nationality and residence of its investors, and the potential tax savings from establishing offshore operations or companies.

Avoiding federal taxes is not easy or inexpensive. The federal tax system is designed to discourage US taxpayers from moving income to tax havens in order to avoid paying taxes. In fact, a

US individual that attempts to avoid US taxes through the use of foreign corporations may end up paying more taxes than if he had organized his company in the United States due to the potential conversion of low-tax capital gains to high-tax dividends or ordinary income. If the company does not have the right characteristics, forming under foreign law could be a disaster. Nevertheless, some companies might be able to take advantage of some planning possibilities.

In the old days, international planning fell into two broad categories: outbound and inbound. Outbound planning is basically a US person establishing a foreign presence or moving technology or operations to a foreign country. Inbound planning is a foreigner coming into the United States. These days, with the mobility of people and technology, international planning is often a combination of inbound and outbound transactions. For example, an e-commerce company might have US founders but can locate its servers anywhere in the world. Its people can work remotely, and its technology can be owned by a domestic or foreign company. A perfectly reasonable structure would be to establish a Delaware parent company that would own foreign corporations to conduct its foreign operations. A wholly owned foreign IP holding company could hold and license technology to the operating companies as illustrated below. This is a commonly used structure and allows the income and value of the intellectual and intangible property to accrue offshore, free of US taxes. What could possibly go wrong?

First and foremost, this is an expensive structure to establish, requiring tax and legal counsel in multiple jurisdictions, as well as physical presence (employees, offices, etc.) in those jurisdictions. Assuming that the company's investors do not mind giving a large chunk of their investment to lawyers and accountants, there are also the business and tax issues to contend with.

Not every entrepreneur can live with the distraction and complexity of managing an international operation. Most startups have their hands full establishing markets and building their products and companies. For this reason, unless the company is

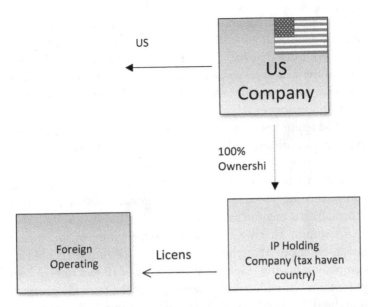

US

US Company

100% Ownershi

Foreign Operating

Licens

IP Holding Company (tax haven country)

in a position to expand very soon, managing a multinational structure may not be worth the hassle. But assuming that the entrepreneur can live with the pain of a complex structure, as is commonly done by well-advised groups, what could go wrong? What might cause the company to be DOA?

An objective of using an IP holding company is the postponement ("deferral") of US taxes on the license value of the intellectual property until those license fees are remitted back (or repatriated) to the US parent company. This is tax *deferral,* not tax avoidance. However, because the IP holding company in the above example will be a controlled foreign corporation (CFC)[30], its "subpart F" earnings[31] will currently be taxable to

---

[30] A controlled foreign corporation ("CFC") is a foreign corporation that is more than 50 percent owned by US shareholders (10 percent US persons). The US shareholders of a CFC must include their pro rata share of the corporation's "Subpart F income" in their income on an annual basis, as if the company declared dividends each year.

[31] "Subpart F Income" is described in IRC section 954 and includes income that is generally easily moved offshore, such as passive income or income from the purchase of a product from a related party and its resale outside of its country of organization.

the US parent company, even if they are not distributed. In order to avoid that adverse result, the IP holding company must be in a country that has a high tax rate (which defeats the purpose of the structure) or must be engaged in an active licensing business, which requires something more than the passive holding and licensing of IP.

The requirement of an active licensing business implies foreign people, offices, and so forth, and that costs money. Given that all the group gets from this is tax deferral—and not tax exemption—the company must determine that the costs of compliance are worth the benefit of deferral and then hope that it actually has income to defer.

Assuming that we can meet those requirements, the next task is to ensure that the transfer of the IP to the IP holding company is tax free. Generally, a transfer of IP to a foreign corporation is a taxable event, meaning that the tax code pretends that the IP has been sold at its fair market value. Without proper structuring, this transaction could actually accelerate the recognition of gain instead of deferring it. The two ways of avoiding this result are to either form the IP holding company at inception so that the IP is developed offshore and not transferred to a foreign corporation, or "sell" the IP in an actual sale very early in the company's life at a low value. This latter option at least limits the tax on formation to a relatively small amount, but the valuation may be subject to IRS attack if the company is very successful very soon. Thus, a professional valuation is advised in this case to establish the value at the time of sale.

As should now be very apparent, the benefit of a US-owned IP holding company is somewhat limited (deferral, not exemption) for many companies, and the costs are somewhat high (sale, valuation, formation, active foreign business). Skip a step in this process, and you end up with a company that has a built-in tax liability. It may not be the end of the world, but it is just another cost for no good reason.

The other issue that the US-owned IP holding structure presents is the effect of withholding taxes. To be effective, the IP holding company should be organized in a tax haven country, and the operating companies would typically be organized in a developed country that taxes its citizens and residents. In that case, theoretically, the payment of the license fees would be deductible by (and reduce the income of) the operating company and be tax free to the recipient IP holding company. This tax arbitrage does not work very well if the license fees or royalties are taxable or subject to withholding, as is often the case.

Most industrialized countries impose withholding taxes on the payment of royalties by its residents or for the use of IP in their jurisdiction. Here in the United States, we often get relief from foreign withholding taxes under income tax treaties that the United States has negotiated with its trading partners. Tax haven countries do not have income tax treaties with the United States; thus, the license fees or royalties will be subject to withholding at rates of up to thirty percent. In that case, again, the benefit of the structure is lost.

Sophisticated structures get around this result by the strategic use of treaty countries or converting what would have been royalties (subject to withholding) to business income (not subject to withholding). These structures typically involve finding ways to treat the IP holding company as engaged in an active trade or business.

One such way is by subcontracting to an operating affiliate. Under the tax code, a branch is treated as a separate CFC in certain circumstances, resulting in all of the income of the branch being treated as subpart F income taxable to the US owner. Current regulations provide criteria for avoiding this result and allow the earnings of the foreign company to remain nontaxed until repatriation, but the rules in this area are subtle and complex.

In the above examples, the parent company is incorporated in the US and forms offshore subsidiaries to hold IP and conduct foreign operations. Sometimes founders consider forming the parent company offshore, often in a tax haven jurisdiction, with the objective of removing their entire business from the US tax net.

While all of the industrialized world knows and accepts the Delaware corporation (meaning a corporation organized under Delaware law), US investors and contracting parties may be wary of foreign corporations. In fact, many US investors would consider a foreign corporation to be riskier as an investment because of the relative uncertainty of foreign law.

If investors are in a company's plans, forming an offshore company might sufficiently chill investor interest so that, all other things being equal, the company's domestic competitor gets funded instead of you. If, however, the company's investors are not averse to investing in a foreign corporation, incorporating offshore may be advantageous taxwise. Companies that will not be more than fifty percent US owned have more flexibility with regard to international planning, since they need not deal with the Subpart F rules (but remain subject to the PFIC rules discussed above).[32] Those companies may be advised to form a foreign, rather than domestic, parent corporation.

Services Companies—Another Model. Brian walked into my office a few years ago with his great idea. He had already done some homework by Googling and talking to tax lawyers, and he was determined to avoid US taxes by doing business through a Bermuda corporation. Brian was willing to place all of his business operations offshore. Other than a reasonable salary to Brian (which would be taxable by the United States because Brian is a US citizen), all of the income could remain and grow free of US tax. Because Brian's business involved the provision of services by employees, he could place those employees in a foreign country under a corporation organized under the laws of that country and avoid US tax on that foreign corporation's earnings. Eventually, the income would be taxed in the United

---

[32] If the foreign corporation is a passive foreign investment company (PFIC), then the US shareholders must include their pro rata shares of passive income in their income, whether or not it is distributed. A foreign corporation is a PFIC if 75 percent or more of its gross income for the taxable year is passive or if at least 50 percent of its assets during the taxable year produce passive income or are held for the production of passive income.

States when paid back to Brian, but in the meantime, he was able to defer that tax and use the earnings to grow the business rather than pay taxes. In Brian's case, the metrics were right for an offshore company.

Chapter 9

Preparing for Exit

From 1904 to 1908, 241 companies entered the US automobile business. Some were based on steam, some burned ethanol, and some burned gasoline. By 1929, three companies controlled 80 percent of the US market. Of the ones that did not make it, many, we can assume, were acquired by bigger players, and bigger players provided their shareholders with liquidity by selling shares on a public exchange. In other words, the successful companies had successful exits.

How soon should you start preparing for an exit? Immediately. Nothing lasts forever, and there will come an optimal time to sell the company. Perhaps the technology is changing, and the founders need to take what they have to the next level. More often, there will be a wave of consolidation in the industry while the bigger players position for market and technical supremacy by buying their competition. Sometimes, it is that the management team is ready for new challenges (or retirement), and the company's goodwill asset will decrease significantly if not sold.

Thinking about selling something before it is even built is a hard thing to do, and in fact, successful companies are built on sustainability and not a quick profit. An investor will not want to hear that the founders are so intent on cashing out that they might not have the resolve to stay with the company long-term if necessary. However, some companies simply do not prepare for their eventual sale because it seems so remote or they view their companies as something they will be with until death does them part. Death comes pretty quickly for those companies, especially when there is an awkward pause after the investors ask about the "exit plan."

While aiming for the quick flip may not indicate a great company, no investor wants to be stuck in an investment that will never become liquid. Eventually the company will be pressured to sell, either by its investors, its board, or its management. Thus, knowing this on the front end makes it easier to plan, and there are a few things that a company can do as a legal matter to make sure its sale or other exit is not delayed or undermined.

Below are a few lessons learned about M&A and what to expect, how to prepare, and what not to do. Some of these companies can serve as good examples; the others as horrible warnings.

Lesson 1: Act Your Age

I first met Dean and Jan in the mid-1990s when they were working out of a dingy warehouse in the East Bay. Dean was technical, and Jan was a marketing genius. Together, they founded their tech company on money obtained from mortgaging their homes. The first few years were tough, and it seemed we had to negotiate every legal bill because they just did not have much money.

Because of their hard work and expertise, the company became very profitable with no outside funding. Although they were making plenty of money by the mid-2000s, the founders remained excessively frugal, and when I suggested that they were big enough that they needed to spend $25,000 on a tax planning transfer pricing study (a drop in the bucket for a company that was worth between $50 million and $100 million by that time), they decided to forego the expense and take their chances that they would not be audited. Similarly, rather than pay some foreign taxes on products that passed through foreign countries, they took an extremely aggressive approach that relied heavily on a strategy of not getting caught.

The list went on and on—they continued to cut corners and take shortcuts wherever they could, even when the dollars they were saving would not have been material. There was always a 100 percent chance that a sophisticated acquirer and their Big Four accountants would eventually discover the problems and punish them in valuation, and that is in fact what happened.

Their middle-market investment banking team did an excellent job preparing a "book" and finding them suitors, and they received a letter of intent (LOI—an offer) of $105 million. It was an excellent offer at the top end of the market value. More importantly, the company had outgrown its managerial capabilities, although the people in charge would never admit it. They accepted the offer, and due diligence commenced.

My clients were about to discover a fundamental rule of M&A practice—the seller's negotiating leverage goes steadily downhill from the moment the LOI is signed. If a buyer walks from a deal, it may not be a big problem from the buyer's perspective (other than lost time and fees), but it is a huge issue for the seller. The stigma of a busted deal is hard for a seller to shake. They must go back into the market and convince another buyer that whatever the problem was that spooked the first buyer has been fixed. This is why a seller should strive to not give a buyer any reason to get cold feet.

It took the buyer's diligence team about a nanosecond to find the compliance problems. Despite the size, the seller had acted like a mom-and-pop shop, surprisingly unsophisticated to this publicly traded buyer, and "sloppily run," as the in-house general counsel described it. Nevertheless, it was still a good deal for all, and the parties agreed to address these issues by taking the costs of fixing their problems out of the purchase price.

The next loose thread that caused their exit to unravel was an inaccurate inventory count. Against the advice of their accountants, they never bothered to implement accounting controls that would have been appropriate for a company their size. The resulting error in inventory went right to their income statement. I argued that the acquirer was buying a company, not a balance sheet, but the acquirer—a publicly traded company—was very focused on numbers, since the numbers would raise their market cap and set a value for the company. They would have to revise their offer to adjust for the bad financials.

The tax problems and the bad numbers were a lot for the buyer to take. The buyer had by that time lost faith in the company's CFO (who was bargain priced, by the way), and even though both sides had spent months negotiating the agreement, the buyer reduced its offer by $10 million.

My guys had a tough choice to make. They could turn down the offer and hope that they could go back into the market. They would now be seen as "damaged goods" in the sense that they were unable to close and would have to convince a new buyer that whatever problems caused the first deal to crater had been dealt with. The process would take a lot of time. Their outside M&A law firm had run up a $500,000 bill that they would not want to pay. They really did not have a lot of good choices, and shortly before midnight on the date that the LOI would have expired, they signed at the lower purchase price. Nobody celebrated that night, and I did not say, "I told you so."

If there is a moral of the story, it is that start-up companies have an unknown constituency (their future buyer) that is far more precise and demanding than they are. At some point, a company must start conducting its business like its potential acquirers in order to avoid being punished in valuation on exit.

Lesson 2: To Delay is To Deny

My client company grew at a crazy pace almost from the beginning. The company culture was manic—the stereotypical Diet-Coke-and-M&Ms-24/7, fast-paced start-up. There was never enough time for anything, and it was a challenge to ensure that the company maintained important corporate documentation.

Because it was a start-up, money was an issue, and like every other start-up, this company promised generous option packages to its employees. The only trouble was that it never found the time to get around to actually adopting an option plan and issuing those options. Then one day, a letter of intent landed on its doorstep. For all the reasons described above, it was the right time to sell. Consolidate or die. And since they now had a liquidity event, they came to me to document the promised option grants.

The problem, as we now know, is that although they promised to grant options years earlier, they never actually did it, and that meant that the options would have to be granted at the current fair market value. Because there was a pending letter of intent, that fair market value could not be too far from the price at which the company would sell. By definition, that meant that the optionees would get very little on a sale since the options were only worth the difference between the value of the underlying stock and the strike price. And then—like almost every company back then—they asked if they could backdate the options to secure the lower strike price.

Of course, by now, everyone had heard that backdating is bad—criminal even. The practice created problems because some executives would date their option exercises on the date that the stock price was lowest, even though the option might have really been granted at a later date when the strike price was higher. This meant that they would have to pay less money to exercise the option. The practice resulted in skewed financials because the financial statements would not pick up the option exercise expense and would not comply with tax rules (which require incentive stock options to be granted at fair market value).

Before some high-profile companies got into hot water and people went to jail over backdating, private companies did it all the time. And they were not shy or secretive about it—nobody seemed to see the harm in the practice, and it was almost as if there were no IRS rules to worry about. I worried about it plenty, however, and I always advised my clients that they simply could not backdate—whether they were public or private. First, the practice would destroy ISO status, which would be a bad thing for most employees. Second, if the option were granted at a "deep discount," it would be deemed exercised on grant, resulting in immediate taxable income to the grantee. In addition, under current law, Code section 409A would impose additional penalties on discounted options. And finally, backdated documents are simply false.

My start-up company client had the good sense to take my advice on the backdating issue (which was later borne out by the backdating scandals of the large companies), but that left them with the problem of their employees having a bunch of worthless options. Fortunately, we were able to fashion a "carve out" plan, which meant that we would just give a portion of the proceeds of sale to select employees who were employed on the date of sale. Although we found a work-around, it would have been more elegant to have been able to use our option plan to accomplish their objectives. The lesson is not to delay since, as facts change, the company's ability to do things will become increasingly restricted.

Lesson 3: If It Sounds Too Good To Be True …

Sight-In was one of my oldest clients. They had a software service platform that allowed them to grow exponentially along with the popular enterprise software that they supported. They knew, however, that it was only a matter of time before the bigger players would figure out their market and take it over. They had to grow it fast and then sell it to a multibillion-dollar company. Growing fast, however, meant cash flow issues, and they could not keep up that type of growth forever. The time to sell came shortly after the turn of the century, when the software service world was past worrying about the millennium and could turn its attention to new problems.

My founder, Don, was not an educated man, but he was self-made. Since he left high school, he had been fending for himself in a variety of industries. His gift was sales, and he had a talent for gathering the right talent and then packaging and selling their expertise. He had built his company from nothing to a company that was worth $20–25 million. At least, that is what it was worth according to almost all of the top-tier, middle-market bankers and brokers that we had consulted. All but one, that is. The company's sole investor strongly recommended that the founder talk to his investment advisor, who we will call Bob.

Bob had a small organization in Marin County that claimed to focus on software companies. One Sunday afternoon, I was summoned by Don to attend a meeting with Bob to discuss his possible engagement by the company. I had never heard of Bob before, but I did know and had been interfacing with the reputable brokers that the founder had been using. We met Bob at the investor's home in San Francisco, and Bob came prepared and "loaded for bear."

He had spreadsheets and charts showing that he could get the founder $70–90 million for his company. Never mind that the reputable brokers had all valued the company at a fraction of that, Bob said. He would negotiate an "earnout,"[33] he continued, that would triple the sales price. I was somewhat amused by the whole snake-oil presentation and did not say much, although Bob anticipated that I would see through him and spent much of the meeting attacking me for not believing his hype. Bob told the founder that he needed to use Bob's lawyer to make sure he got the best deal. Because Bob was so much better than all the other brokers, he required a higher contingent fee, and, by the way, a $500 hourly fee, payable regardless of outcome.

I waited until the ride back to Palo Alto to give Don, the founder, my impressions of Bob, which were not favorable. It seemed to me that if they hired Bob for an hourly fee to sell the

[33] An earnout is a form of contingent consideration in which the amount payable to the sellers is partly based on achieving post-close performance goals.

company for three times what it was worth, they would end up with a large bill from Bob and no sale. I assumed that my founder would be able to see through the hype, given what an obvious scammer Bob was and what an accomplished salesman Don was. Unfortunately, I did not notice the spell that Bob had cast on Don by repeatedly mentioning the sum of $90 million and giving this unrealistic amount false credibility with mathematical models and jargon. I was flabbergasted to learn that the founder wanted to engage Bob. Because he held a majority of the shares and board seats, Don could do so. I advised him that Bob was so obviously unqualified that he would face potential liability to his shareholders after Bob screwed up his sale (at $500 per hour). While Don was concerned that I had such a strong view, in the end, greed got the better of him. They hired Bob and, by necessity, fired me. Can you guess what happened next?

Bob did in fact find a buyer for the company, but the potential buyer did not value the company anywhere near what Bob said they would. Bob's Soviet-style negotiating eventually led to the buyer backing away from the deal entirely with—big surprise—the company owing Bob about $500,000 in hourly fees. Result: no sale, big bill. That might have been bad enough, but things were about to get worse.

Don came back to me at that point, sufficiently chastened, to regroup. Then, September 11 happened, and any deal that might have happened three months earlier was off the table forever. The company failed soon afterward, and all of the company's value went away. The investor threatened litigation, and the founders ended up broke and sued—all because of Bob and his promise of three times what the company was worth. My client's greed cost him and his investors $25 million.

The lesson here is obvious, but from a legal standpoint, the question might be "What could they have done about it?" The problem with this company was not a misguided founder or a slick sales broker—it was governance. The company's board had to engage the broker, and if the company would have had an independent board, it might have acted more rationally. In this case, the party that would have normally insisted on a real board of directors was the investor—and he, oddly, did not ask for those protections. This was a case where the investor truly did need protection from the founder; in fact, the founder needed protection from the founder.

The moral of the story is that founders will sometimes do crazy things. One of the things that made them great founders may have been that they were mad as hatters, which is great at start-up, but at exit, some adult supervision is needed.

Lesson 4: Who Cares About Taxes?

A start-up company is a closely held company, at least in the beginning. A closely held company does not have only corporate-level legal issues. It has joint corporate- and shareholder-level issues, especially when it comes to taxes. Unfortunately, most start-ups do not think about taxes, and especially shareholder-level taxes. This comes up in a couple of contexts.

The benefits of an S corporation over a C corporation are discussed above in an earlier chapter. Nevertheless, I have seen so many companies organized as C corporations when they should have been S corporations that I cannot use a single example. The all-too-common scenario is as follows:

1. The organizers form the company as a corporation and do not make an S election because the founders plan to sell preferred stock to an institutional investor, which would terminate the S election anyway.

2. The company ends up needing less money than expected, so it issues convertible debt instead of an equity security.

3. Then, the founders sell the company and exit without ever doing the equity round.

As discussed above, the tax cost of not making the S election can be huge. We have to live with two levels of tax in the case of a C corporation that issues preferred stock, but those taxes are a gift to the federal and state governments in the case of a company that never issues any preferred stock.

What should they have done? When in doubt, make the S election.

The second place in start-up-company-land where taxes matter is in connection with shareholder-level estate and gift-tax planning. The basic concept is simple—since gift taxes are based on the value of the gifts, it is less expensive, tax-wise, to gift shares early in a company's life when the values are low than later when values are high. In addition, there are numerous vehicles designed to leverage gifts by "splitting" the interests. For example, a few basic estate-planning techniques are described below.

GRATs, GRUTs, and GRITs. A grantor retained annuity trust (GRAT) allows a stockholder to give property to children or trusts for children while retaining an annuity interest, the value of which reduces the taxable gift—sometimes to zero. A stockholder establishes a GRAT by making an irrevocable donation into a trust. Each year, the trust pays back to the stockholder a specified percentage of the value of the stock given to the trust (this retained interest is called an "annuity"). The annuity payment is often made by transferring some of the same stock back to the shareholder—but this time at its then-current (and hopefully higher) value. A grantor retained unitrust (GRUT) and a grantor retained income trust (GRIT) are similar to the GRAT, except that the annual amount paid back to the stockholder is calculated differently. With any of these techniques, however, at the expiration of the trust term, the remaining trust principal is either distributed to beneficiaries or held and managed in further trust for the benefit of the stockholder's children or other predetermined beneficiaries.

These types of trusts are designed to save gift and estate taxes by reducing the value of the taxable "gift" to the discounted present value of the expected remainder as prescribed by IRS regulations. For example, if a founder wants to gift $2 million worth of stock to a beneficiary, he or she could either make a direct gift and pay gift tax based on its $2 million value as of the date of gift or he or she could make the gift through one of the foregoing types of trusts and pay tax on the current discounted value of a gift that passes at some point in the future (i.e., the present value).

Defective Grantor Trust. Closely related to the GRAT is the concept of a defective grantor trust. This type of trust structure anticipates a "sale" of stock to a trust that is treated as owned by the grantor for income tax purposes (thus, it is referred to as "defective"—a misnomer). The trust, however, is respected for gift and estate tax purposes, so the property is moved out of the grantor's taxable estate. Though often more effective than a GRAT, GRIT, or GRUT, and although founded on well-established statutory authority, legal precedents, and IRS rulings, the defective grantor trust technique is not specifically sanctioned by statute. Thus, as a tax matter, it can be viewed as a riskier technique.

Annual Exclusion Gifts. Finally, current law (as of this writing) allows an annual exclusion from gift tax for gifts of up to $13,000 annually per donee, per donor. In addition, by electing "gift splitting" among spouses, a donor and his spouse can gift $26,000 per year to any individual without gift tax consequences.

With all of these techniques, the trick is that they are most effective when done early while valuations are low. Waiting until the eve of a deal to implement these strategies is better than not doing it at all but will not take full advantage of the lower valuations that can be supported early in a start-up company's life.

One DOA problem that this sort of planning creates arises when the corporate and estate-planning lawyers act at cross-purposes. For example, for corporate law reasons, the company may value its stock at one value while the estate planners use a completely different value. While there is often a tension between corporate-level- and individual-shareholder-level planning, the tension can become expensive in some areas and disastrous in at least one. That one is where the corporation has elected to be an

S corporation but a stockholder has transferred his shares to a trust that does not qualify as an S corporation shareholder.

US residents and citizens, as well as certain types of trusts, may be S corporation shareholders. Entities and nonresident aliens may not hold stock in an S corporation. A trust can hold S stock if it is a "grantor" trust, electing small business trust (ESBT) or qualified Subchapter S trust (QSST). A "grantor" trust is a trust over property that is treated as owned by the grantor for income tax purposes, either because the grantor retains certain powers over the trust administration or control over the property inside the trust.

In order for a trust to be a QSST, it must meet the following requirements:

a. There is only one income beneficiary, and he or she is a US citizen or resident.

b. All income of the trust is required to be distributed currently to the one income beneficiary.

c. All corpus distributions must go to the one beneficiary.

d. The beneficiary's income interest must terminate at the earlier of the beneficiary's death or trust's termination.

e. An election to be treated as an eligible S corporation shareholder must be made.

An ESBT is similar to a QSST but can have more than one beneficiary, and the income can be distributed or accumulated. The ESBT trust is taxed on the income related to the S corporation at the highest individual tax rate on ordinary income and 20 percent on long-term capital gains. A special election is also required for an ESBT.

A trust can have two different components and still qualify as a QSST trust. For example, part of the trust consisting of assets other than the S corporation stock can be treated as a simple trust while the QSST portion of the trust will be treated similarly to a grantor trust. This type of situation requires a bifurcated type of trust income tax return. The trust return will report the income and deductions for all assets, excluding the S corporation, and it will separately report the S corporation income and deductions similarly to a grantor trust return.

The income beneficiary of the QSST signs the consent required on IRS Form 2553. In addition, the trust beneficiary must make a QSST election within sixteen days and two months of the date the stock was transferred to the trust or sixteen days and two months from the beginning of the first S corporation year. If it is a newly elected S corporation, the special QSST election can be made as part of the S election on Form 2553. It is important to note that if the QSST election is not made, the S corporation election would be revoked.

Every once in a while, an uninformed stockholder will transfer some of his shares to his nonresident alien relative, a trust that does not meet the above requirements, or a family limited partnership. This action will automatically "blow" (or terminate) the company's S election, meaning that corporation may have unreported taxes, interest, and penalties for all years that it should not have been filing as an S corporation. The IRS liberally allows corrective action for inadvertent terminations of the S election, but some problems cannot be fixed, such as a transfer to a party that does not want to rescind. This problem is often discovered in due diligence and will kill a stock acquisition and give pause in an asset deal (due to successor liability concerns). Estate planning should never be done in a vacuum or without regard to business-level issues.

Lesson 5: Keys to the Kingdom

"I just want enough out of this deal to buy a private airplane," my client said. He owned just over fifty percent of a company that had a signed an LOI for a sale at $325 million valuation. He would have plenty for his airplane if it closed.

The problem was that the forty percent shareholder was the CEO, and forty percent of $325 million was not enough for him. He wanted the company to go public. We all knew that what he really wanted was to be the CEO of a public company. He was all ego. It was ironic that this CEO was now in charge of negotiating the sale of the company in a deal we all knew he did not want.

My client had enough shares to control the board and to replace the CEO whenever he wanted to. He had not done so, mostly to avoid confrontation. Relations had become strained over the years as their business goals diverged. They had been in this company together for almost fifteen years now, and my client wanted out while the CEO wanted to continue to grow the company. It did not take a legal genius to see that the guy who was negotiating the deal should not be the guy who most wanted it to fail, but now here we were, LOI in hand, documents in play.

The deal dragged on and on. Every little issue seemed to be a deal breaker. I sent several strong letters reminding the CEO of his fiduciary obligations. His lawyer sent strong letters back assuring us that he was doing his job. In the meantime, the price started to drop. The buyer was a savvy financial buyer and knew that the longer our company was in play, the less it would be worth. My client watched the valuation go from $325 million to $250 million to $200 million, and then at that point, the credit markets collapsed in 2008, and our debt-financed deal went away altogether, along with my client's airplane dreams. We were now damaged goods.

It took a good two years to regroup and reposition the company for sale. Fortunately, the company did fire its CEO after that earlier debacle—personal feelings aside—and the company did go back to market after the stigma of a cratered deal subsided. Sale price: $180 million—a little more than half of what they would have gotten if they had acted more boldly sooner.

Lesson 6: You Can't Get There from Here

Like a lot of start-ups, my new client company used its stock as its currency. Instead of paying cash, which was scarce, it paid employees in stock, which was easily printed. When it came time to exit, they had close to one hundred stockholders. That normally would not have been a problem since it only takes a majority of shares to approve a merger; however, in this case, the buyer was unsure as to whether they wanted all of the shares of my client. Thus, they proposed using a set of offsetting puts and calls. In other words, they would buy half the shares now and have a right to buy the remaining half a year later. Of course, their endgame was to end up with 100 percent of the company, which would require 100 percent of the stockholders to agree to the sale. The problem was that they could not get 100 percent consent. They could not even *find* 100 percent of the stockholders. The company had consulted other counsel who told them that they could not find a way to do the transaction as proposed. The buyer was intractable—it did not want the company except on its terms. There were no other buyers, at least not at anywhere near that price. The company would have to pass on the $25 million offer that was on the table, or so they were told.

Their former counsel was partly correct—they could not do the transaction as proposed. They could, however, do it the way we proposed.

One of the problems with legal solutions, especially for startup or smaller companies, is the presence of a herd mentality. Just as companies may have a knee-jerk preference for forming as a C corporation, there are several standard "cookie cutter" forms of acquisition that fit 99 percent of all the deals that need to be done. When the deal does not fit the structure, however, the answer is not to trash the deal—the answer is to find a new and sometimes novel structure.

We ended up doing the transaction via a two-step process—one step involving a merger of the corporation into an LLC and the second involving the LLC executing put-and-call agreements. The structure was novel, unique, creative, and devilishly effective at accomplishing the parties' objectives. The moral of the story is to get more than one legal opinion, and get it from someone who knows.

Lesson 7: Too Clever By a Half

Most of my technology company clients start their careers as engineers. As such, they are smart enough to go online and figure out what the law is. They can immediately comprehend even the most complex tax issues. The concept that is much harder for them to grasp is that, as Justice Oliver Wendell Holmes once said, the life of the law is experience, not logic. Thus, they were smart enough to know that their employees would have tax advantages by exercising their options early, but not wise enough to take my advice to discourage that practice. They were smart enough to make an S election, but not experienced enough to get tough S corporation related covenants from their shareholders. They could not conceive of a scenario in which all the shareholders would not all have the same interests in minimizing taxes and signing whatever might be necessary down the road to do so. Why should they protect against the unlikely scenario of a shareholder doing something that would terminate their S election and increase everyone's tax burden?

The answer came on the eve of close of their sale. Because the company was an S corporation, and the buyer had insisted on a special election under Code section 338(h)(10),[34] we were required to get a written consent from each and every shareholder at close. By encouraging early exercise of options, the company had dozens of shareholders, and we obtained that consent from all but one person—a person who had left the company on very bad terms. She had a grudge to bear and the S

---

[34] Under Code section 338(h)(10), a buyer of the stock of an S corporation can elect to treat the stock sale transaction as a sale and purchase of assets, thereby obtaining a fair market value cost basis in those assets. All of the selling shareholders, however, must consent to the election,.

election would make very little difference with respect to her $4,000 worth of stock.

When I called her and asked her to sign our 338(h)(10) consent so we could close and deliver her $4,000 of proceeds, she said that she probably would—she just wanted to check with her lawyer first. When I called back the next day she announced that she had indeed checked with her lawyer, and the price of her consent would be $1,000,000.

Why so much? Because she figured out that although the election would save her a couple thousand dollars in taxes, as structured, the deal could not happen at all without her consent. It was too late to re-structure. She had leverage.

We settled with her for a couple hundred thousand dollars, but the hard lesson is that a company cannot possibly anticipate all the possible scenarios, or chart on a decision matrix all the ways things might work out, so please just take the advice of experience when it is given.

Chapter 10

Choosing Counsel

The first thing to know is that no lawyer in the world can make your company successful, but the wrong lawyer can cause it to fail. In that sense, picking a lawyer for your company is a defensive measure. You want to ensure that you find someone who knows the lore as well as the law and has the right kind of experience. Some common mistakes are as follows.

"We Will Help You Get Funded." Lawyers regularly introduce their client companies to VCs and angels, and some law firms use their connections as a selling point in a way that borders on (if not crossing the line into) broker activities. It is perfectly legitimate to factor this into the legal counsel decision, but a little diligence ahead of time might not be a bad idea. Many law firms will expect equity for acting as counsel to an unfunded company. Since equity is forever, you should be sure you have the right firm before engaging with them. For example, does the firm represent or even know the type of investors that your company needs? I have had several clients who needed a few hundred thousand dollars of funding hire very large law firms on this basis only to find out that all of their contacts will only do deals worth tens of millions. That makes sense since large firms handle large transactions and may not be able to do small deals economically. If the firm does not regularly do $100,000 placements, don't expect it to be able to introduce you to investors at that level.

"We Know the VC Community." Here is something you should know about VCs. They are not known for their brand loyalty. VCs use a lot of law firms and constantly seem to be shopping around. As a result, the market for VC-backed deals is competitive, and law firms that focus in that area are regularly pitching to the VCs. More than one entrepreneur has shared with me that he thought his lawyers were just a bit too solicitous to the VC investor, and while I am sure those entrepreneurs were well represented, the fact that the company has those sorts of doubts does not lend itself to a very trusting attorney-client relationship. For example, if your lawyer is advising you to accept a three-year vesting schedule on your previously unvested shares, is it because a vesting restriction truly is market based and reasonable in your case, or is it because he or she would not want to have a reputation in the VC community for being difficult to deal with? If your lawyer makes a big deal about knowing a lot of VCs, make sure he or she understands that you require his or her undivided loyalty, even if he has to step on some VC toes.

"We Are Big and Bad." There are some excellent start-up company lawyers in large firms. There are also some real nitwits in large firms. A national brand is worth very little in this space. For example, a large Boston firm that does East Coast bond deals or Chinese private equity fund formations may not have a clue about start-up company practice. They might also charge you a small fortune while learning it and training their associates to learn it. I have inherited more than one company with a six-figure legal bill from a large firm for what would have been $10,000 of legal work if someone more knowledgeable had paid attention to commercial expectations.

"We Are Cheap." Inexpensive is good, but what I said about expensive, large firms applies to inexpensive small or solo practices. While cost is important to a start-up company, a lack of relevant expertise can cost you your company. While your brother-in-law who works at the district attorney's office might be an excellent lawyer doing whatever it is that he does in his day job, he might not be the right attorney to handle your multimillion dollar M&A exit. There are attorneys who know what they are doing in this space and will work for reasonable fees. Those of us who won't will often make deals, which brings us to …

"Let's Make a Deal." A typical fee for equity deal is to grant the law firm one percent of the prefinancing equity in the company in exchange for $15,000 to $25,000 in fees for up to one year. During the dot-com bubble of the late '90s, that number was typically 2 percent, and some more aggressive firms took up to 5 percent. Those days are probably gone forever, but the concept of equity for fees is still alive and a necessary practice for many companies. It not only conserves cash but aligns the law firm's goals with those of the company (i.e., to get liquid). Similarly, the reluctance of a law firm to defer fees may signify a lack of confidence in the business model.

An outright fee-for-equity deal is less common these days, since many lawyers have been burned—and burned badly. However, it does happen, and there are lawyers who have made more money from their equity than they have practicing law. Lawyers who are that entrepreneurial do not stay lawyers for long, so you may want to consider how much risk you want in a legal advisor if presented with this option a bit too eagerly.

Some commentators have pointed out the conflicts that result when a lawyer works for equity, or simply takes equity in a client. Those relationships, it is argued, put the lawyer in a position of having a self-interest in ensuring that a deal gets done, so that their equity is worth something, even if it may not be the best deal for the client. For example, is a founder being asked to make an expansive warranty or representation with respect to their company? Is the founder being asked to provide a personal indemnity? The lawyer who owns equity benefits from that personal indemnity if the lawyer is a stockholder. This is especially true when the company gets to the stage of being sold. At that point, any personal exposure that the founder assumes will make a deal more likely, and thus directly benefit the lawyer.

In practice these issues tend to be more theoretical than real, and so long as everyone understands the theoretical tensions, deals tend to get done on market terms regardless of the immaterial incentives represented by small grants of equity. Nevertheless, it is a good practice for everyone to be aware of the potential conflicts so that the company can consult independent counsel if desired.

Concluding Words

The previous chapters contain a summary of the most common legal mistakes that entrepreneurs make on their paths to success. Whether it is during formation, financing, or exit, the potential for business-ending mistakes is always present. Most of these mistakes will come up again and again, and none are unforeseeable. The one thing, in fact, that every legal mistake has in common is that they are totally avoidable with the help of competent legal counsel. My hope in writing this book is not to give you a technical legal treatise on the law of start-ups (there are already plenty of books that do that) but instead that you, the start-up entrepreneur, have a sense of the basic issues to watch for and the ways to anticipate and avoid making any legal mistakes. Good luck with your company.

CPSIA information can be obtained
at www.ICGtesting.com
Printed in the USA
FSHW020623110120
65395FS

9 781457 509803